W9-BEI-899

CAREER IDEAS for kids who like COMPUTERS

DIANE LINDSEY REEVES
AND PETER KENT

Illustrations by
NANCY BOND

Facts On File, Inc.

CAREER IDEAS FOR KIDS WHO LIKE COMPUTERS

Copyright © 1998 by Diane Lindsey Reeves

All rights reserved. No part of this book may be reproduced or
utilized in any form or by any means, electronic or mechanical,
including photocopying, recording, or by any information storage
or retrieval systems, without permission in writing from the publisher.
For information contact:

Facts On File, Inc.
132 West 31st Street
New York NY 10001

Library of Congress Cataloging-in-Publication Data

Reeves, Diane Lindsey, 1959–
    Computers / Diane Lindsey Reeves and Peter Kent, illustrations by
Nancy Bond.
      p. cm.—(Career ideas for kids who like)
    Includes bibliographical references and index.
    Summary: Discusses computer-related occupations such as
programmer, online researcher, and systems analyst, and describes
how to prepare for them.
    ISBN 0-8160-3682-9 (acid-free paper)
    1. Computer science—Vocational guidance—Juvenile literature.
[1. Computer science—Vocational guidance.   2. Vocational guidance.]
I. Kent, Peter, 1957– . II. Bond, Nancy, ill. III. Title. IV. Series:
Reeves, Diane Lindsey, 1959–   Career ideas for kids who like.
QA76.25.R44   1998
004'.023'73—dc21   98-5199

Facts On File books are available at special discounts when purchased in
bulk quantities for businesses, associations, institutions, or sales promotions.
Please call our Special Sales Department in New York at 212/967-8800 or
800/322-8755.

You can find Facts On File on the World Wide Web at http://www.factsonfile.com

Text and cover design by Smart Graphics
Illustrations by Nancy Bond

This book is printed on acid-free paper.

Printed in the United States of America

MP FOF 10 9 8 7 6 5

This book is dedicated with love to
my husband, Garon Reeves.
Without your support and encouragement
all this would still be a dream.

—Diane Reeves

ACKNOWLEDGMENTS

A million thanks to the people who took the time to share
their career stories and provide photos for this book:

Elias AbuGhazaleh
Phil Bair
Brenda Dickson Curry
Rachel Drummond
Lowell Hawkinson
Susan Krauss
Ron Kuhl
Victor Kushdilian
Mike Little
Kurt Matthies
John Pemberton
Molly Roberts
Jeni Li Shoecraft
Tim Vann
Will Wright

Also, special thanks to the design team of Smart Graphics,
Nancy Bond, and Cathy Rincon for bringing the
Career Ideas for Kids series to life with their creative talent.

Finally, much appreciation and admiration is due to
my editor, Nicole Bowen, whose vision and attention
to detail increased the quality of this project in
many wonderful ways.

CONTENTS

MAKE A CHOICE!

You're young. Most of your life is still ahead of you. How are you supposed to know what you want to be when you grow up?

You're right: 10, 11, 12, 13 is a bit young to know exactly what and where and how you're going to do whatever it is you're going to do as an adult. But, it's the perfect time to start making some important discoveries about who you are, what you like to do, and what you do best. It's the ideal time to start thinking about what you *want* to do.

Make a choice! If you get a head start now, you may avoid setbacks and mistakes later on.

When it comes to picking a career, you've basically got two choices.

CHOICE A

Wait until you're in college to start figuring out what you want to do. Even then you still may not decide what's up your alley, so you graduate and jump from job to job still searching for something you really like.

Hey, it could work. It might be fun. Lots of (probably most) people do it this way.

The problem is that if you pick Choice A, you may end up settling for second best. You may miss out on a meaningful education, satisfying work, and the rewards of a focused and well-planned career.

You have another choice to consider.

CHOICE B

Start now figuring out your options and thinking about the things that are most important in your life's work: Serving others? Staying true to your values? Making lots of money? Enjoying your work? Your young years are the perfect time to mess around with different career ideas without messing up your life.

Reading this book is a great idea for kids who choose B. It's a first step toward choosing a career that matches your skills, interests, and lifetime goals. It will help you make a plan for tailoring your junior and high school years to fit your career dreams. To borrow a jingle from the U.S. Army—using this book is a way to discover how to "be all that you can be."

Ready for the challenge of Choice B? If so, read the next section to find out how this book can help start you on your way.

HOW TO USE THIS BOOK

This isn't a book about interesting careers that other people have. It's a book about interesting careers that you can have.

Of course, it won't do you a bit of good to just read this book. To get the whole shebang, you're going to have to jump in with both feet, roll up your sleeves, put on your thinking cap—whatever it takes—to help you do these three things:

- 💡 **Discover** what you do best and enjoy the most. (This is the secret ingredient for finding work that's perfect for you.)

☼ **Explore** ways to match your interests and abilities with career ideas.
☼ **Experiment** with lots of different ideas until you find the ideal career. (It's like trying on all kinds of hats to see which ones fit!)

Use this book as a road map to some exciting career destinations. Here's what to expect in the chapters that follow.

GET IN GEAR!

First stop: self-discovery. These activities will help you uncover important clues about the special traits and abilities that make you *you*. When you are finished you will have developed a personal Skill Set that will help guide you to career ideas in the next chapter.

TAKE A TRIP!

Next stop: exploration. Cruise down the career idea highway and find out about a variety of career ideas that are especially appropriate for people who like computers. Use the Skill Set chart at the beginning of each entry to match your own interests with those required for success on the job.

MAKE A COMPUTER DETOUR!

Here's your chance to explore up-and-coming opportunities in computer science as well as the fields of systems analysis, engineering, and other technical areas.

Just when you thought you'd seen it all, here come dozens of computer science ideas to add to the career mix. Charge up your career search by learning all you can about some of these opportunities.

DON'T STOP NOW!

Third stop: experimentation. The library, the telephone, a computer, and a mentor—four keys to a successful career planning adventure. Use them well, and before long you'll be on the trail of some hot career ideas.

WHAT'S NEXT?

Make a plan! Chart your course (or at least the next stop) with these career planning road maps. Whether you're moving full steam ahead with a great idea or get slowed down at a yellow light of indecision, these road maps will keep you moving forward toward a great future.

Use a pencil—you're bound to make a detour or two along the way. But, hey, you've got to start somewhere.

HOORAY! YOU DID IT!

Some final rules of the road before sending you off to new adventures.

SOME FUTURE DESTINATIONS

This section lists a few career planning tools you'll want to know about.

You've got a lot of ground to cover in this phase of your career planning journey. Start your engines and get ready for an exciting adventure!

GET IN GEAR!

Career planning is a lifelong journey. There's usually more than one way to get where you're going, and there are often some interesting detours along the way. But, you have to start somewhere. So, rev up and find out all you can about you—one-ot-a-kind, specially designed you. That's the first stop on what can be the most exciting trip of your life!

To get started, complete the two exercises described below.

WATCH FOR SIGNS ALONG THE WAY

Road signs help drivers figure out how to get where they want to go. They provide clues about direction, road conditions, and safety. Your career road signs will provide clues about who you are, what you like, and what you do best. These clues can help you decide where to look for the career ideas that are best for you.

Complete the following statements to make them true for you. There are no right or wrong answers. Jot down the response that describes you best. Your answers will provide important clues about career paths you should explore.

Please Note: If this book does not belong to you, write your responses on a separate sheet of paper.

On my last report card, I got the best grade in _____.

On my last report card, I got the worst grade in _____.

I am happiest when _____.

Something I can do for hours without getting bored is _____.

Something that bores me out of my mind is _____.

My favorite class is _____.

My least favorite class is _____.

The one thing I'd like to accomplish with my life is _____.

My favorite thing to do after school is _____.

My least favorite thing to do after school is _____.

Something I'm really good at is _____.

Something that is really tough for me to do is _____.

My favorite adult person is _____ because _____.

When I grow up _____.

The kinds of books I like to read are about _____.

The kinds of videos I like to watch are about _____.

GET SOME DIRECTION

It's easy to get lost when you don't have a good idea of where you want to go. This is especially true when you start thinking about what to do with the rest of your life. Unless you focus on where you want to go, you might get lost or even miss the exit. This second exercise will help you connect your own interests and abilities with a whole world of career opportunities.

Mark the activities that you enjoy doing or would enjoy doing if you had the chance. Be picky. Don't mark ideas that you wish you would do, mark only those that you would really do. For instance, if the idea of skydiving sounds appealing, but you'd never do it because you are terrified of heights, don't mark it.

Please Note: If this book does not belong to you, write your responses on a separate sheet of paper.

- ❑ 1. Rescue a cat stuck in a tree
- ❑ 2. Visit the pet store every time you go to the mall
- ❑ 3. Paint a mural on the cafeteria wall
- ❑ 4. Run for student council
- ❑ 5. Send e-mail to a "pen pal" in another state
- ❑ 6. Survey your classmates to find out what they do after school
- ❑ 7. Try out for the school play
- ❑ 8. Dissect a frog and identify the different organs
- ❑ 9. Play baseball, soccer, football, or _____ (fill in your favorite sport)

❏ 10. Talk on the phone to just about anyone who will talk back

❏ 11. Try foods from all over the world—Thailand, Poland, Japan, etc.

❏ 12. Write poems about things that are happening in your life

❏ 13. Create a really scary haunted house to take your friends through on Halloween

❏ 14. Recycle all your family's trash

❏ 15. Bake a cake and decorate it for your best friend's birthday

❏ 16. Sell enough advertisements for the school yearbook to win a trip to Walt Disney World

❏ 17. Simulate an imaginary flight through space on your computer screen

❏ 18. Build model airplanes, boats, doll houses, or anything from kits

❏ 19. Teach your friends a new dance routine

❏ 20. Watch the stars come out at night and see how many constellations you can find

❏ 21. Watch baseball, soccer, football, or _____ (fill in your favorite sport) on TV

❏ 22. Give a speech in front of the entire school

❏ 23. Plan the class field trip to Washington, D.C.

❏ 24. Read everything in sight, including the back of the cereal box

❏ 25. Figure out "who dunnit" in a mystery story

❏ 26. Take in stray or hurt animals

❏ 27. Make a poster announcing the school football game

❏ 28. Think up a new way to make the lunch line move faster and explain it to the cafeteria staff

❏ 29. Put together a multimedia show for a school assembly using music and lots of pictures and graphics

❏ 30. Invest your allowance in the stock market and keep track of how it does

❏ 31. Go to the ballet or opera every time you get the chance

❏ 32. Do experiments with a chemistry set

❏ 33. Keep score at your sister's Little League game

❏ 34. Use lots of funny voices when reading stories to children

❏ 35. Ride on airplanes, trains, boats—anything that moves

❏ 36. Interview the new exchange student for an article in the school newspaper

❏ 37. Build your own treehouse

❏ 38. Help clean up a waste site in your neighborhood

❏ 39. Visit an art museum and pick out your favorite painting

❏ 40. Play Monopoly® in an all-night championship challenge

❏ 41. Make a chart on the computer to show how much soda students buy from the school vending machines each week

❏ 42. Keep track of how much your team earns to buy new uniforms

❏ 43. Play an instrument in the school band or orchestra

❏ 44. Put together a 1,000-piece puzzle

❏ 45. Write stories about sports for the school newspaper

❏ 46. Listen to other people talk about their problems

❏ 47. Imagine yourself in exotic places

❏ 48. Hang around bookstores and libraries

❏ 49. Play harmless practical jokes on April Fools' Day

❏ 50. Join the 4-H club at your school
❏ 51. Take photographs at the school talent show
❏ 52. Make money by setting up your own business—paper route, lemonade stand, etc.
❏ 53. Create an imaginary city using a computer
❏ 54. Do 3-D puzzles
❏ 55. Keep track of the top 10 songs of the week
❏ 56. Train your dog to do tricks
❏ 57. Make play-by-play announcements at the school football game
❏ 58. Answer the phones during a telethon to raise money for orphans
❏ 59. Be an exchange student in another country
❏ 60. Write down all your secret thoughts and favorite sayings in a journal
❏ 61. Jump out of an airplane (with a parachute, of course)
❏ 62. Plant and grow a garden in your backyard (or windowsill)
❏ 63. Use a video camera to make your own movies
❏ 64. Get your friends together to help clean up your town after a hurricane
❏ 65. Spend your summer at a computer camp learning lots of new computer programs

❑ 66. Build bridges, skyscrapers, and other structures out of LEGO®s

❑ 67. Plan a concert in the park for little kids

❑ 68. Collect different kinds of rocks

❑ 69. Help plan a sports tournament

❑ 70. Be DJ for the school dance

❑ 71. Learn how to fly a plane or sail a boat

❑ 72. Write funny captions for pictures in the school yearbook

❑ 73. Scuba dive to search for buried treasure

❑ 74. Recognize and name several different breeds of cats, dogs, and other animals

❑ 75. Sketch pictures of your friends

❑ 76. Pick out neat stuff to sell at the school store

❑ 77. Answer your classmates' questions about how to use the computer

❑ 78. Draw a map showing how to get to your house from school

❑ 79. Make up new words to your favorite songs

❑ 80. Take a hike and name the different kinds of trees, birds, or flowers

❑ 81. Referee intramural basketball games

❑ 82. Join the school debate team

❑ 83. Make a poster with postcards from all the places you went on your summer vacation

❑ 84. Write down stories that your grandparents tell you about when they were young

CALCULATE THE CLUES

Now is your chance to add it all up. Each of the 12 boxes on these pages contains an interest area that is common to both your world and the world of work. Follow these directions to discover your personal Skill Set:

1. Find all of the numbers that you checked on pages 9–13 in the boxes below and X them. Work your way all the way through number 84.
2. Go back and count the Xs marked for each interest area. Write that number in the space that says "total."
3. Find the interest area with the highest total and put a number one in the "Rank" blank of that box. Repeat this process for the next two highest scoring areas. Rank the second highest as number two and the third highest as number three.
4. If you have more than three strong areas, choose the three that are most important and interesting to you.

Remember: If this book does not belong to you, write your responses on a separate sheet of paper.

ADVENTURE	ANIMALS & NATURE	ART
❏ 1	❏ 2	❏ 3
❏ 13	❏ 14	❏ 15
❏ 25	❏ 26	❏ 27
❏ 37	❏ 38	❏ 39
❏ 49	❏ 50	❏ 51
❏ 61	❏ 62	❏ 63
❏ 73	❏ 74	❏ 75
Total: _____	Total: _____	Total: _____
Rank: _____	Rank: _____	Rank: _____

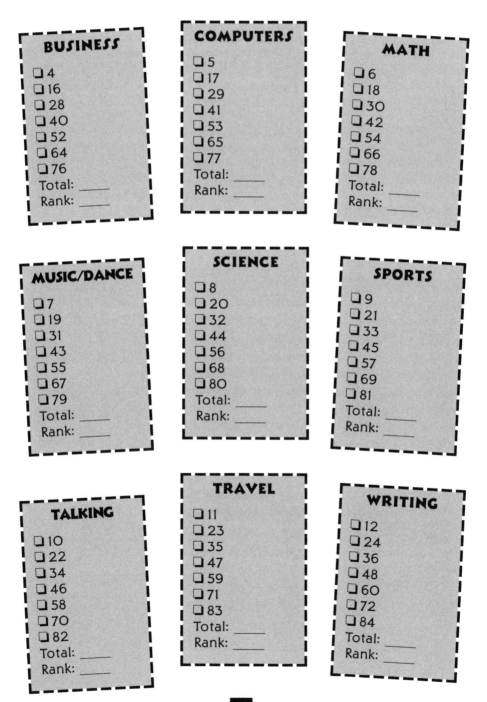

BUSINESS

❑ 4
❑ 16
❑ 28
❑ 40
❑ 52
❑ 64
❑ 76
Total: _____
Rank: _____

COMPUTERS

❑ 5
❑ 17
❑ 29
❑ 41
❑ 53
❑ 65
❑ 77
Total: _____
Rank: _____

MATH

❑ 6
❑ 18
❑ 30
❑ 42
❑ 54
❑ 66
❑ 78
Total: _____
Rank: _____

MUSIC/DANCE

❑ 7
❑ 19
❑ 31
❑ 43
❑ 55
❑ 67
❑ 79
Total: _____
Rank: _____

SCIENCE

❑ 8
❑ 20
❑ 32
❑ 44
❑ 56
❑ 68
❑ 80
Total: _____
Rank: _____

SPORTS

❑ 9
❑ 21
❑ 33
❑ 45
❑ 57
❑ 69
❑ 81
Total: _____
Rank: _____

TALKING

❑ 10
❑ 22
❑ 34
❑ 46
❑ 58
❑ 70
❑ 82
Total: _____
Rank: _____

TRAVEL

❑ 11
❑ 23
❑ 35
❑ 47
❑ 59
❑ 71
❑ 83
Total: _____
Rank: _____

WRITING

❑ 12
❑ 24
❑ 36
❑ 48
❑ 60
❑ 72
❑ 84
Total: _____
Rank: _____

What are your top three interest areas? List them here (or on a separate piece of paper).

1. _____

2. _____

3. _____

This is your personal Skill Set and provides important clues about the kinds of work you're most likely to enjoy. Remember it and look for career ideas with a skill set that matches yours most closely.

TAKE A TRIP!

Quick! How many
jobs can you think of
that don't use comput-
ers? Chances are your list will be pretty short because computers have completely revolutionized the workplace.
Almost every business from gas stations and restaurants to
airlines and government agencies use computers to perform very important on-the-job functions.

This section profiles some of the major career options in
computers today; however, this list is just the beginning.
And chances are that the career you'll have in computers in
the next several years doesn't even exist right now. That's
how fast the technology industry changes.

Use these ideas as a first step to discovering the computer career that's right for you.

As you read about each career, imagine yourself doing the job, and ask yourself the following questions:

☼ Would I like it?
☼ Would I be good at it?
☼ Is it the stuff my career dreams are made of?

If so, make a quick exit to explore what it involves, try it out, check it out, and get acquainted!

Buckle up and enjoy the trip!

A NOTE ON WEBSITES

Internet sites tend to move around the Web a bit. If you have trouble finding a particular site, use an Internet browser to find a specific website or type of information.

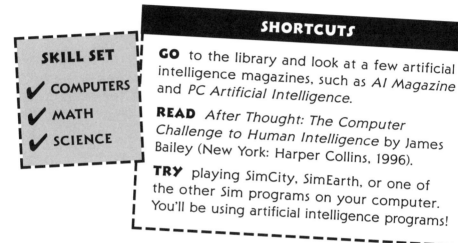

Artificial Intelligence Scientist

SHORTCUTS

SKILL SET

✔ COMPUTERS

✔ MATH

✔ SCIENCE

GO to the library and look at a few artificial intelligence magazines, such as *AI Magazine* and *PC Artificial Intelligence*.

READ *After Thought: The Computer Challenge to Human Intelligence* by James Bailey (New York: Harper Collins, 1996).

TRY playing SimCity, SimEarth, or one of the other Sim programs on your computer. You'll be using artificial intelligence programs!

WHAT IS AN ARTIFICIAL INTELLIGENCE SCIENTIST?

First things first. Before you can consider a career in artificial intelligence, you'll need to understand what artificial intelligence, or AI, is. In a nutshell, AI is the application of computer science and other sciences to make machines imitate what people do by programming intelligent behavior.

That means that artificial intelligence scientists are, in effect, teachers. The difference between them and your teachers at school is that their students are computers instead of people. Their job is to teach computers to think like very smart humans.

Artificial intelligence has been around for a while—it began in the late 1950s. But until recently the only way to work in this exciting field was to be involved in research because AI promised more than it could deliver for a long time. These days AI is at work in many walks of life—from medicine to the food industry—and the field is growing fast. For instance, AI systems are used by Nabisco to bake their chocolate chip cookies. A computer has been programmed to examine every aspect of the process: It checks how much of each ingredient is going into each batch, whether the temperature is just right for baking consistently crisp cookies, and so forth. When something in the process gets out of kilter. the computer has to figure out how to fix it—pronto.

This sort of task used to be handled by humans, the human brain being the only "computer" that could examine so many different aspects of a process and keep them running smoothly simultaneously. Now people working in AI are learning how people make complicated decisions and are teaching computers to do the same. Another exciting frontier for AI is in the medical field. One AI application in the works involves programming computers to diagnose certain diseases. This process involves a medical professional describing a patient's symptoms to the computer. The computer asks questions based on the original information, considers the possibilities, provides a diagnosis, and prescribes a course of medicine or treatment. Obviously, technology like this could have a major impact on health care programs all over the world.

AI projects like these and others start with some very detailed analysis of the problem and proposed solutions. This process is called "modeling" and involves creating a computer model of the entire process. Models are complex mathematical equations that define how a process works (for example, how cookies get baked or how the body reacts to infectious disease). The model isn't complete until it is as close to reality as possible. Once an accurate model has been created, AI scientists must "teach" the computer how to react to changes in a useful manner.

If you enjoy playing computer games, you may already be using AI programs without realizing it. SimCity and SimEarth are great examples of relatively simple AI programs. These games are models—of the earth or a fictional city. They're not perfect, of course (planets and cities are incredibly complex systems), but they are "working" models. Add energy to the planet, and you'll get some kind of reaction; create an earthquake in the city, and you'll get another. Add your input, and the computer game directs the development of the planet accordingly.

You may have guessed by now that artificial intelligence is an especially demanding computer field. The work involves very complex thinking and the most sophisticated computer skills—there isn't much room for novices here. AI scientists have to know their stuff, starting with the most basic programming courses that are often offered at the high school level and moving toward "object oriented" languages such as Java. Eventually, AI scientists must learn how complex computer systems function and must work with lots of advanced software programs, such as voice recognition, computer vision, language translation programs, and so on. Anything that humans do is fair game for an AI application. Now, if someone could just program a computer to do homework. . . .

TRY IT OUT

COMPUTERIZED COOKIES

If Nabisco can use computers to bake chocolate chip cookies, so can you!

First, find a recipe for chocolate chip cookies. If your family doesn't have a favorite, just look on the back of a bag of chocolate chips. Read the recipe carefully.

Now go back and think of all the different ways people might interpret the instructions. Add all the mistakes people might make, for instance, adding too much sugar or not enough butter. Maybe they get called to the phone and leave the cookies in the oven too long or the stove isn't adjusted correctly and the temperature is lower than it should be. Perhaps they live in Denver, a mile above sea level, where baking works differently than it does elsewhere. Perhaps the chef didn't close the oven door completely after checking on the cookies. As you can see there are quite a few ways to change the process.

Think of as many possibilities as you can and list them on one-half of a sheet of paper. On the other half, write instructions that can get the process "back on track." Putting the cookies back in for so many minutes, adjusting the temperature, adding a particular quantity of another ingredient are a few possible solutions.

If you find that you really don't know how to fix a particular problem, ask someone. (You may even find that there's a toll-free phone number listed on the chocolate chip package that you can call with questions).

SMART WEBSITES

Artificial intelligence is essential to computer games. Computer games such as chess, bridge, or solitaire all have a little intelligence programmed into them. So go on-line and investigate the idea of becoming an AI engineer.

The World Wide Web provides a number of artificial intelligence games. These are usually programs that try to hold a conversation with you. You ask a question, for example, and the program answers you. You read the question, then respond, and the computer responds again. These can be fun, although you'll often find that the computer seems to be thinking about something other than the conversation, because it frequently gives you answers that don't seem to match your questions! Well, we warned you—AI has a long way to go!

Try some of these games.

- ☼ Ask the Milk Mystic at http://www.whymilk.com/mystic/
- ☼ Julie from Phoenix Quest at http://taz.cs.ubc.ca/julie/
- ☼ Barry DeFacto at http://fringeware.com/bot/barry.html

You can also go to Yahoo! (http://www.yahoo.com) and search for *artificial intelligence games.* You'll find all sorts of sites related to the use of AI in games, including more advanced games.

VISIT MARVIN MINSKY AND MIT
Visit Marvin Minsky's website (http://www.ai.mit.edu/people/minsky/minsky.html). Minsky is an AI pioneer, and his website contains interesting articles such as "Why People Think Computers Can't" and "Alien Intelligence." The site also has links to AI research groups.

You could visit the Massachusetts Institute of Technology AI lab (http://www.ai.mit.edu/), where you'll find scores of links to AI research sites. Learn what has been done in AI so far, and what people are working on now.

And the *PC Artificial Intelligence* magazine site (http://www.pcai.com/pcai/) has lots of useful information too. To subscribe write to P.O. Box 30130, Phoenix, Arizona 85046.

LEARN AN AI PROGRAMMING LANGUAGE
There's actually an AI language designed for children of all ages: It's called Logo. This programming language is similar to LISP, the original AI language. You can get Logo for free, for both PCs and Macs. To order try the *PC Artificial Intelligence* magazine site at http://www.pcai.com/pcai/New_Home_Page/ai_info/pcai_logo.html or The Great Logo Adventure at http://www.cyberramp.net/jmul/.

CHECK IT OUT

American Association for Artificial Intelligence (AAAI)
445 Burgess Drive
Menlo Park, California 94025-3442
E-mail: info@aaai.org
Web: http://www.aaai.org/

IEEE Systems, Man, and Cybernetics Society
IEEE Member Services
P.O. Box 1331
445 Hoes Lane
Piscataway, New Jersey 08855-1331
Phone: 800-678-4333
E-mail: services@ieee.org
Web: http://www.isye.gatech.edu/ieee-smc/

GET ACQUAINTED

Lowell Hawkinson, Artificial
Intelligence Scientist

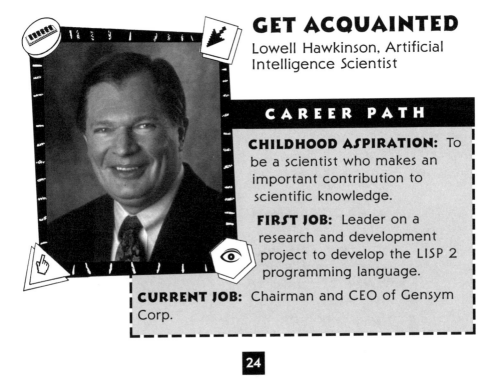

CAREER PATH

CHILDHOOD ASPIRATION: To be a scientist who makes an important contribution to scientific knowledge.

FIRST JOB: Leader on a research and development project to develop the LISP 2 programming language.

CURRENT JOB: Chairman and CEO of Gensym Corp.

AN EARLY START

Lowell Hawkinson's involvement in AI goes back a long way, almost to the beginning of the technology. AI research began in the late 1950s at the Massachusetts Institute of Technology (MIT); Hawkinson appeared on the research scene while studying physics at Yale in 1962. He had met someone who was working with the early AI pioneers and became so fascinated with the subject that he decided to build his own version of LISP, the original AI programming language. In fact, LISP AI began to take up most of his time as the excitement of this new world displaced interest in his original studies.

Hawkinson's first job in AI was developing LISP for the U.S. Department of Defense, under the auspices of ARPA (the Advanced Research Projects Agency, the same group that set up the Internet). Then, after several years of involvement in various software development projects, he became a research associate at MIT's Laboratory for Computer Science, working on natural language and natural language processing, two important areas of AI research.

INTO THE REAL WORLD

Since then he's spent 13 years working in the artificial intelligence industry, bringing AI out of the universities and into the cookie factories, automobile plants, and the Internet. For a while Hawkinson worked for LISP Machines, Inc., an AI company founded by researchers from MIT. Then in 1986, he and several other people from LISP Machines founded Gensym, the company that Hawkinson heads today. This company calls itself "a leading supplier of software and services for intelligent systems that help organizations manage and optimize complex dynamic processes." That may sound complicated, but it could also be described as "we help DuPont make fibers, Motorola manage communication satellites, and Nabisco bake cookies."

THE FUTURE OF COMPUTING

Hawkinson believes that AI is the future of computing: "This is where computers are going. There's a lot of work to be done in the 21st century to make ordinary systems more and more intelligent." AI will play an essential role in making computers understand our voices, for instance, or recognize what they see through video cameras. But not only has AI got an exciting future, it's already had a big impact on the computer business. "AI has been a spawning ground for many advanced technologies," he says. "Graphical window systems, for instance, came from within the context of AI research projects."

The Internet is an example of a problem waiting for an AI solution." Everyone understands that information coming through the Internet, for example, will be pervasive," he remarks. "We're going to see incredible amounts of information available. raw data. What will set apart successful organizations will be the intelligent use of the data. Artificial intelligence is going to help us deal with what's been called 'info-glut.'" AI will be used to create more intelligent devices, machines that will help us handle far more information than we could ever hope to deal with by ourselves.

Computer Game Designer

SHORTCUTS

GO to Yahoo! on the World Wide Web (http://www.yahoo.com/) and search for *computer game*. Be prepared to spend hours exploring the thousands of links you'll find!

READ *The Great Logo Adventure* by Jim Muller (Madison, Ala.: Doone Publications, 1997).

TRY playing a computer game. While you are playing, analyze what is happening and try to imagine what the designer was trying to get you to do.

SKILL SET

✔ ADVENTURE
✔ MATH
✔ COMPUTERS

WHAT IS A COMPUTER GAME DESIGNER?

You mean, some people get paid to create computer games? Yep! Computer game designers enjoy the dream job of almost every kid who loves computers. Creating computer games can be very challenging and a whole lot of fun.

In the early days of computer games, a single person could create a game. These days, teams are used to create them. In some cases, huge teams—similar to the sorts of teams that make movies—are required to put together sophisticated computer games. In fact, high-budget computer games cost more to create than low-budget movies. (Wing Commander reportedly cost $17 million to make!)

The computer game designer develops and, in many cases, programs the game. The designer is often working alongside artists, writers, programmers, music and sound design staff, and even actors in some cases. Designing a computer game can be fascinating work; there's much more to it than meets the eye. It begins with the basic idea behind the game. Then there's the object of the game—what the player must do to

win—and the obstacles of the game—what the computer does to keep the player from winning. The graphics and sound effects are also a big part of the entire creative package. In short, a lot of work must happen before the play begins!

There are basic requirements for a career in computer games: a creative imagination and a background in computer programming. Don't let the second requirement scare you off. Programming doesn't have to be complicated. Think of it as playing with building blocks. You learn a number of simple commands first. Then you combine and link the commands to build something—one block at a time.

One way to test your aptitude for computer programming is to learn how to use a programming language called Logo. This language is designed as a first experience for kids but is sophisticated enough to use for years. If you decide that computer games are in your future, you'll eventually want to learn more "mainstream" programming languages, such as Visual Basic, C, or C+ +.

Learning about computer graphics and file formats can be helpful too. Computer games are similar to multimedia in that they require the use of a large number of different programs, media types, and file formats, which often leads to problems. The more familiar you are with multimedia, the more easily you'll be able to deal with the problems when they arise.

One more thing: Math can be very helpful too. Math is used to create algorithms, step-by-step problem-solving procedures that are essential to game programming. So as you pay a little more attention in math class, just think of it as learning the skills you'll use in your computer game career.

TRY IT OUT

LEARN THE LINGO

Logo, the kid's programming language, provides a very quick way to get involved in programming. It allows you to begin controlling the actions of people and animals within a few minutes of beginning work. You don't need to study the language for months before you can do anything, you can get started almost immediately.

A number of versions of Logo are available, some of which are free. Your school may already have Logo, or you can download it from the Internet. Try these sites to get a copy of Logo.

- ☀ The Kids and Computers Web Site at http://www. magma.ca/~dsleeth/
- ☀ Softtronics/MSWLogo at http://www.softronix.com/
- ☀ *PC Artificial Intelligence* magazine at http://www.pcai. com/pcai/New_Home_Page/ai_info/pcai_logo.html
- ☀ The Great Logo Adventure at http://www.cyberramp. net/~jmul/

START A COMPUTER GAME CLUB

Start a computer game club with a few friends. What for? To create a club library so that members can borrow new games. Everyone shares their computer games because it's fun and perfectly legal as long as the game is only being used on one computer at a time. Make sure to set rules and insist that everyone abide by them to avoid problems. This way, everyone gets to play with the latest and greatest games without having to buy all of them.

At your club meetings, talk about the various games and find out what the other kids think about them. Put your heads together and try to figure out how each game works. Then think up ways to improve the games.

Once the group has existed for a while and has a regular membership, try writing to the game companies and asking for demo software. Your club's expertise can help them work the kinks out of a particular game and figure out the best way to reach their audience—other kids just like you.

Contests are another exciting way to keep the club going. Encourage members to learn Logo and use it to create simple games for each other to try out. Great practice and great fun. What are you waiting for?

READ AND PLAY

Get the inside story on the game industry by reading magazines such as:

Computer Gaming World
P.O. Box 57167
Boulder, Colorado 80323-7167
http://www.computergaming.com/

GamePro
P.O. Box 55528
Boulder, Colorado 80323-5528
http://www.gamepro.com/

Next Generation
P.O. Box 54682
Boulder, Colorado 80232-3682
http://www.next-generation.com/

For a good overview of the game-developing process, you may want to read a book or two on the subject. One possibility is *Teach Yourself Game Programming in 21 Days* by Andre Lamothe, (Indianapolis: Sams Publishing, 1994).

The World Wide Web is another great source for information about computer games, including lots of mailing lists and news groups. Investigate news groups such as gamers-l; GAMES-L; alt.binaries.mac.games; rec.games.computer.quake.editing; rec.games.computer.stars; and hundreds more. To find these discussion groups, go to http://www.liszt.com/ and search for the words *computer game.*

CHECK IT OUT

Computer Game Developers' Association (CGDA)
960 North San Antonio Road, #125
Los Altos, California 94022
E-mail: member-services@cgda.org
Web: http://www.cgda.org/

GET ACQUAINTED

Will Wright, Computer Game Designer

CAREER PATH

CHILDHOOD ASPIRATION: To be an astronaut, architect, or pilot.

FIRST JOB: Never had a real job.

CURRENT JOB: Chief designer and director at Maxis Corporation.

A DIFFERENT KIND OF MODEL

Will Wright always loved models—model ships, model planes, model tanks. He enjoyed learning about the machine he was building and putting together the model. So when he started using a computer—an Apple II, in 1980—he was delighted to discover that it was possible to build models inside the computer. In those days, computer games were very primitive, but Wright realized that games were really models, little toy worlds, and he taught himself to program so that he could build these little toy worlds. Instead of building toys with balsa wood or plastic, he began to build them with lines of computer code.

SIDETRACKED COLLEGE DEGREE

Wright spent five years in college—studying architecture, mechanical aviation, and various other subjects—but he never quite got around to finishing his degree. He became infatuated with computer games instead of his studies.

He learned to program on the Apple II but decided that wouldn't take him very far because thousands of people could already program on the Apple II. When the Commodore 64 computer arrived on the scene late in 1981, he saw his chance to get in right at the start of a new computer market. He bought a Commodore 64 immediately, then locked himself away in a room for a few weeks.

He learned how to program it as quickly as he could; then he wrote a game, a "stupid" game, he says. It was called Raid on Bungling Bay. He sold it to a large software company—Broderbund—and the game sold reasonably well in the United States. Broderbund licensed the game to Nintendo in Japan, where it sold 700,000 copies! With the royalties from Nintendo in hand, Wright didn't need to look for a job; he could continue programming.

Raid on Bungling Bay is a game in which helicopters bomb islands. Wright discovered something interesting while writing this program; he enjoyed creating the islands much more than he enjoyed bombing them. He discovered that, for him at least, the research required to create the game was more fun than creating the game itself.

In 1985 he began work on a program called SimCity, a computer model of a city. In 1987 he met Jeff Braun at a pizza party and described the game he was working on; together they founded Maxis, hired a small group of programmers, and published the game two years later. Since that time SimCity has sold over 5 million copies.

MILLIONS OF COPIES LATER . . .

Maxis has sold 2 million copies of other Sim products: SimEarth, SimAnt, SimCopter, SimTower, and plenty more. These are far more than simple "shoot-em-up" games; they require a great deal of planning and research to create. In fact, Wright spent two years researching ants while working on SimAnt. These programs are models of real-world systems—cities, planets, colonies, and so on—and they incorporate basic artificial intelligence technology.

Wright does a little programming these days, but he has a staff of programmers to do the bulk of the work. "For me, the research is the best thing," he says. "I still like programming and it's essential that I still understand programming to a detailed level, but most of my time is spent in designing games."

Creating computer games can be tremendously stressful, but it can also be tremendously satisfying. Wright comments, "The hardest part, by far, is the last two months of a project; 90 percent of the effort is done in the last 10 percent of the time, getting the bugs out and finishing off details. You don't get much sleep during that time, but there's a great feeling of satisfaction when the product's finally out the door."

Computer Programmer

SKILL SET

✔ COMPUTERS

✔ MATH

✔ SCIENCE

GO visit a computer show, look at the programming displays, and talk to all the programmers you can find.

READ *Computer Programming in Basic the Easy Way. An Introduction to Computer Programming* by Douglas Downing (Hauppauge, N.Y.: Barron's, 1989).

TRY recording a macro in a word processor such as Word for Windows. Then look at the finished macro and see if you can understand the commands. (Ask your teacher how to record macros.)

WHAT IS A COMPUTER PROGRAMMER?

A computer programmer is a person who "writes" computer programs. The programmer sits down at a computer terminal and types in a set of instructions known as source code. Source code is just ordinary text in a file like one you'd create in any word processing program.

When the instructions are complete, the programmer compiles the program; that is, he uses a compiler program to take the text instructions and convert them into a program file, such as the .exe and .com files you see when you look in Windows File Manager or Windows Explorer. This program file is the file that actually does the work, the file that is sold to customers.

Of course, the instructions the programmer writes into the text file are not just plain English words. They're commands that are part of a programming language, and there are hundreds of different languages. You've probably heard of some of them: Visual Basic, FORTRAN, Pascal, BASIC, Assembly, C, C+ +, Java, and Ada. (Ada is named after Ada Lovelace, the world's first computer programmer who, believe it or not, died in 1852. She created programs for Charles Babbage's analytical machine, which he never quite got around to building.) There are lots of different programs for many different purposes, and most programmers understand several languages.

In fact, most programmers learn several languages because they really *enjoy* it. This is not the sort of career to get into just because you need a way to make a living; it's a "love it or hate it" type of thing, and good programmers really love programming. Programmers generally find that they enjoy the creative process of building something from scratch, spending hours on end at the keyboard. On one hand, it can be very exciting and satisfying to watch a program develop on the screen. On the other hand, there's often a lot of drudgery involved with programming. Even the most enthusiastic programmers find some tasks that they dislike intensely, such as testing the program to get the bugs out of it or documenting the program so that other people can use it.

In one way programming is often a team effort. Many projects involve hundreds of programmers handling very specific aspects of the overall program. In another way, programming can also be a very solitary task: it's just the programmer and the computer. If you think you're more of a "people person," this may not be the job for you.

If you think you might enjoy programming, however, the only way to find out is by trying it. Take programming classes at school. Learn Logo at home or in the school computer lab (see under Artificial Intelligence Scientist and Computer Game Designer to find out how to obtain a copy of Logo). Try as many programming languages as you can.

Once you graduate from high school, you'll want to consider pursuing a computer science degree in college—that's probably the easiest way into the career. However, many very skilled and highly respected programmers have no degree, or they have a degree in a completely unrelated subject. This is the sort of career in which many people are self-taught.

Actually, once you start trying to learn how to program, the decision of whether or not to be a computer programmer will become pretty obvious. If you catch on fast, enjoy it, and find it difficult to tear yourself away from the computer, you'll know you've caught the programming bug.

TRY IT OUT

FIND A MACRO LANGUAGE

Macro languages can be found built into many different programs. If your computers at school have Microsoft Word for Windows, for example, you'll find that you can write macros that carry out certain procedures on word processing documents. These macros are written in a special scripting language called WordBasic.

Ask your computer teacher which programs have scripting or macro languages, then try to find the documentation for these languages. Read through the documentation and then write a few simple macros. For instance, write a macro that searches a word processing document for straight quotation marks (') and changes them to curly quotation marks ("and").

You can also take a look at the program's existing macros. Most programs will have a library of macros already built, and you can open these and read the instructions. Keep the instruction manual handy for details.

PROGRAMMING 101

Millions of PCs produced over the last 15 years came with some form of BASIC installed, generally GW-Basic, Qbasic, or MS-BASIC. BASIC is a very simple programming language; the name stands for *Beginner's All-purpose Symbolic Instruction Code*. It major advantage is that it's widely available, and it's a good toy to play with for a while. Many programmers will say that it's not good to use BASIC for too long, though, as it teaches a few bad programming habits.

Ask your computer teacher which computer has a copy. Qbasic has been shipped on PCs for several years now, including MS Windows computers. You can usually start Qbasic by going to the DOS prompt, typing *qbasic*, and pressing "Enter."

It's very simple to get started, especially if you have a book about BASIC (there are lots of books on this subject). You can also use these websites: Qbasic Tutorial (http://www.alphalink.com.au/alain/qbas) and Qbasic for Beginners (http://www.geocities.com/SiliconValley/Heights/ 5976).

PROGRAM DISSECTION

According to experts, computer programming is one of the fastest growing professions around. Have you every wondered what all these newly employed programmers are doing? What about those projects that involve hundreds of programmers—what could all those people possibly be doing?

Good questions! Here's how to find out some answers. First, go to a computer store and make a list of all the different kinds of programs that you find. Make a note of what each program is used for. Find one that looks particularly interesting or complicated and look on the back of the box for a toll-free phone number or an Internet address.

Call or e-mail the company and ask to be put in touch with one of the programmers. Tell them that you are interested in becoming a programmer some day and are trying to find out more about the profession. Ask them to describe how the team of programmers worked together to produce the program you are inquiring about. Find out how many different people were involved and what their roles were.

After your discussion, make a chart that illustrates the process. Highlight the part of the process in which you would have liked to have been involved.

If you happen to already know someone who's a programmer, you can ask them to help you with this project.

CHECK IT OUT

Association of Information Technology Professionals (AITP)
505 Busse Highway
Park Ridge, Illinois 60068
Phone: 800-224-9371
E-mail: 70430.35@compuserve.com
Web: http://www.aitp.org/

National Association of Programmers (NAP)
P.O. Box 529
Prairieville, Louisiana 70769
Phone: 888-335-5646
E-mail: info@naponnet.org
Web: Use a browser to search for NAP's website.

GET ACQUAINTED

Victor Kushdilian, Computer Programmer

CAREER PATH

CHILDHOOD ASPIRATION: To be a scientist working in the space program.

FIRST JOB: Assistant to an electrical engineer, working on printed circuit board layout.

CURRENT JOB: President of SportsWare.

STARTING WITH HARDWARE

Victor Kushdilian always enjoyed math and science, so as a kid he thought he'd like to work on the space program. That's why he earned a degree in electrical engineering at the University of Southern California. However, his first job after graduating was not in engineering but with IBM (International Business Machines) as a computer technician. He worked on computer hardware for seven or eight years.

Large companies such as IBM often provide training opportunities for their employees, and Kushdilian made the most of it. He learned about systems software, operating systems, and mainframe programming. Eventually he began programming as part of his job.

He was also programming at home, just for fun. Kushdilian has always been a creative person. He enjoys building things and is often doing things around his house. He found that programming is just another form of creating something. You build a program, watch it grow, and see it come alive.

COMPUTERIZED FOOTBALL

He began by creating small database programs. A database program is simply a program that stores data in a structured form so that the data can be searched for and retrieved quickly. Many computer programs are essentially database programs—address books and contact managers, e-mail programs, mail-merge programs, and so on—and many others include some form of database. Working with databases is a good skill for a programmer to have.

A database needs data, of course, so Kushdilian found a favorite source of data he could use while experimenting with these programs: football statistics. He began by creating a database that would store football stats and allow him to find any piece of information he wanted. But then he took things a step further and created a fantasy football program. Fantasy football, played by millions of Americans, is a game in which players create make-believe teams using real players; that is, they pick the real-life players they'd *like* to have on their teams, then track each player's performance during the game season. To do that, they have to collect a lot of information, and most people write down all this information on paper. But a computer database is an ideal tool for the job!

After writing the program for his own use, Kushdilian realized that if *he* found it useful, somebody else probably would too. So in 1990, almost on an impulse, he put an ad in a small football magazine offering copies of his program for $50. He got a few calls, but when he made his first sale, he really wasn't prepared. He wasn't set up to accept payments, do accounting, or ship programs. He ran out and bought an invoice book and some office supplies, made a diskette, and sent it out.

That ad sold 30 copies of the program over the first year. Kushdilian called all 30 customers and asked them how he could make the program even better. Then he set about improving the program by adding new functions. All along he'd still been working at IBM, but in 1992 he borrowed a little money, quit his job, and started a full-fledged business.

KEEP MOVING

Today he finds thousands of new customers each year and sells thousands more program upgrades. And he's branched out. No longer does he just sell fantasy football programs, but he has expanded his line of products to include fantasy hockey, fantasy basketball, and fantasy baseball. Each program uses the same basic database structure as the original fantasy football program, though it is customized for each sport. Kushdilian is doing business on the Internet too, and a significant portion of his new business comes that way. You can visit his site at http://www.sportsware.com/.

Kushdilian plans to expand his business, adding new products and services and exploring new technologies. "It's a nonstop race," he says. "You have to keep running. and have to run faster, just to stay where you are. Technology moves so quickly. If you don't keep up, you'll fall behind!"

Hardware Engineer

SKILL SET

✔ MATH

✔ SCIENCE

✔ COMPUTERS

SHORTCUTS

GO visit Yahoo! and see the wide range of hardware that companies are working on. Go to http://www.yahoo.com; then go to the following links: Business and Economy; Companies; Computers; and Hardware.

READ *Fun With Computer Electronics: Build 20 Electronic Projects with the Same Type of Chips Used Inside Computers* by Luann Colombo and Conn McQuinn (Kansas City, Mo.: Andrews & McMeel, 1996).

TRY putting together complex 3-D puzzles. That's precisely the kind of skill you'll need as a hardware engineer.

WHAT IS A HARDWARE ENGINEER?

Behind all the glitzy graphics and amazing capabilities of the latest software is the hardware that makes it happen. And behind all the hardware are the engineers whose ideas and hard work have made it all possible.

All the exciting things you can do with a computer, such as simulate travel in space and chat with people around the world, are brought to you courtesy of hardware engineers who have created the tools that run the software. Computer hardware includes the "guts" of a computer—all the pieces that make a computer work its magic.

Hardware engineers can be found in every area of the computer business. They design the chips that are at the very heart of the computer as well as the processors that are doubling in speed every 18 months. They design the boards that the processors sit on, known as motherboards. They design disk drives, video screens, the big tape drives used by mainframe computers, the networking components used to

connect different computers together, the CD-ROM drives, modems, keyboards, mice, printers, and scanners. The list goes on and on.

And the list continues to grow: machines that "print" models of machine components in 3-D—that is, they create three-dimensional objects in a waxlike substance, machines that create smells, machines that print 3-D models of people's faces. These are all real technologies under development right now.

Hardware engineers have a wide range of roles. They are involved in the design of components at the very first level, creating the circuit diagrams that will be used to build the new component. They are also involved in development, building prototypes and modifying the item to get it to work properly. They're also involved in testing the component; they make sure that the item will perform properly in any condition it's likely to work under, and they make sure that it's durable enough to last.

Hardware engineering is a very demanding career. There's an awful lot to learn, and an ability to apply advanced levels of math and science is required to do well in this career. You'll need a college degree in a subject such as electrical engineering. Many people in this business have advanced degrees too.

Not everyone who loves computers is cut out for this type of work. But for those who are, the rewards can be substantial—both in salary and job satisfaction. Hardware engineers are very well paid, and as it requires a lot of work to enter the profession, it seems likely that demand for hardware engineers will always be high.

If you are interested in becoming a hardware engineer, take all the math and science courses you can. If your school teaches electronics, study that too. You need to enjoy solving problems. Hardware engineering is like a very complicated puzzle, combining various components to create a new computer device. Math is an especially critical part of the job. So the better you are at math, the better you'll be as a hardware engineer.

TRY IT OUT

TRY A SCIENCE EXPERIMENT
Find a good electronics book or kit and build something. The following books and book-kit combinations contain electronics experiments in which you actually build an electronic device.

- The *Shocking Science* book and kit (New York: Sterling, 1997).
- *Magnets & Electric Current* in the Super-Charged Science Projects series (New York: Barron's Educational Series, 1994).
- Jim Becker and Davina Parmet's *Build Your Own Telephone Kit* (Philadelphia: Running Press, 1997).

When working on kits and experiments, follow the instructions very carefully: one small mistake and whatever it is you're building won't work! If you find this sort of experiment tedious or boring, you won't do well in hardware engineering. But if you think it really fun, perhaps you should investigate more.

READ ABOUT NANOTECHNOLOGY

Hardware engineering seems to be moving toward a really exciting technology: nanotechnology. This technology is more theory than fact right now, but the developments are happening rapidly. With nanotechnology, industries will be able to create things by plugging atoms together, instead of taking a large portion of some material and breaking it down, which is what, in essence, is done today. With nanotechnology, we'll be able to build from the ground up by plugging one atom into another.

Nanotechnology promises to change the world of technology completely. Creating things will become very fast and very cheap, and we'll be able to create materials and products we can only dream of right now, such as microscopic robots that can move through a blood vessel seeking out viruses, and computers of a completely new type that are much faster and smaller than the ones we have today.

Visit a few nanotechnology websites and see what information is available. Perhaps one day you'll be working with this fantastic new technology.

- Nanotechnology Today at http://nexxus.som.cwru. edu/dept/mids/courses/mids411/mxd41/
- Nanocomputer Dream Team at http://nanocomputer.org/
- *NanoTechnology* magazine at http://nanozine.com/
- Sean Morgan's Nanotechnology Pages at http://www. lucifer.com/~sean/Nano.html

IT'S GOT SOUL

For an idea of the excitement—and stress—involved in creating computer hardware, read *The Soul of a New Machine* by Tracy Kidder (New York: Avon, 1995). Kidder watched a team of about 30 designers, working for Data General in the 1970s, create a new minicomputer, from the early designs to the finished product. Kidder made the story exciting—and won a Pulitzer Prize for his effort.

As you read, keep track of the phases the team went through from start to finish. See if you can identify all the steps between having a great idea and producing a working product.

CHECK IT OUT

IEEE Computer Society
1730 Massachusetts Avenue NW
Washington, D.C. 20036-1992
Phone: 800-678-4333
E-mail: membership@computer.org
Web: http://www.computer.org/

IMAPS (International Microelectronics and Packaging Society)
1850 Centennial Park Drive, Suite 105
Reston, Virginia 20191-1517
Phone: 888-464-6277
E-mail: IMAPS@aol.com
Web: Use a browser to search for their website.

Institute of Electrical and Electronics Engineers (IEEE)
445 Hoes Lane
P.O. Box 459
Piscataway, New Jersey 08855-0459
Phone: 800-678-4333
E-mail: student.services@ieee.org
Web: http://www.ieee.org/

GET ACQUAINTED

John Pemberton, Hardware
Engineer

CAREER PATH

CHILDHOOD ASPIRATION:
To be an engineer after going
through the professional football player phase.

FIRST JOB: Pumping gas and
fixing cars at a gas station
when he was a teenager.

CURRENT JOB: Manufacturing manager for a major
semiconductor company.

A HIGH-TECH WORLD

John Pemberton works in a laboratory that operates 24 hours
a day, 7 days a week. His staff consists of more than 500
technicians who work different shifts making computer chips.
He's responsible for more than $1 billion worth of equipment
and oversees a work environment that is 1,000 times clean-
er than a medical operating room. Everyone who enters the
super-sterile laboratory must wear head-to-toe gear known
as bunny suits. The technicians wear helmets so that even the
air they breathe is filtered.

The product being manufactured is so tiny that you can't
even see it without the help of a high-powered microscope.
Each technician works on a specific part of the process by
using very specialized tools. The entire process of manufacturing a computer chip takes about 50 to 60 days.

A JUGGLING ACT

When his sons ask him what he does at work, Pemberton likes
to tease them by saying he sits in meetings all day. As manager of the team that produces these high-tech components,

Pemberton certainly has lots of reasons to call a meeting. He says his work can basically be summed up in four words: productivity, planning, forecasting, and troubleshooting.

Productivity involves finding ways to make the most and best microchips with the least amount of resources. It means figuring out systems that are as quick and as efficient as possible.

Planning involves keeping things running smoothly and dealing with any number of issues that pop up when running an operation that involves hundreds of people and billions of dollars worth of high-tech equipment.

Forecasting is what keeps Pemberton's team one step ahead of the competition. He has to know how many chips to produce in order to keep the world's computers working in top condition.

Troubleshooting involves finding solutions to any problem that might hinder the successful production of microchips.

COLLEGE TO CAREER

Pemberton has actually worked for the same company ever since he graduated from college. He went to Iowa State University with the intention of becoming a chemical engineer. While there, he became interested in industrial engineering because of the way it combined engineering with management. He used his time in college to find out more about what he wanted in his career.

At an on-the-job learning experience at an antifreeze manufacturing factory, Pemberton discovered that he didn't want to do dirty work. Instead he started looking for opportunities to work in a clean, environmentally friendly manufacturing environment. When he took some computer courses in college and really enjoyed them, he decided that the electronics industry might be just the place to start looking for his ideal job.

Right before he graduated, he sent résumés out to various electronics companies. He received an offer from one of the industry "giants" but chose to join the up-and-coming firm he still works with now. It turned out to be a good choice for

Pemberton, as he's had plenty of opportunity to advance his career as a hardware engineer.

A JUMP START

Pemberton credits his father and grandfather with nurturing the skills he needed to be successful as an engineer. His dad worked with Pemberton when he was a child, giving him help in math and problem-solving and teaching him how to apply mathematical principles to real-life situations. His grandfather, who worked in the heating and air-conditioning business, spent time with Pemberton, showing him how to build things and put things together. It was through these experiences that he gained an appreciation for the mechanical world and discovered how much he enjoyed it.

WORDS OF ADVICE

1. **Math.** Master it and you can do anything in engineering.
2. **Work.** Get a job while you're young and you'll discover some interesting things about yourself, the value of money, and your priorities in life.
3. **Learn.** Pay attention in high school. It's tough to make up for lost time in college.

Internet Systems Administrator

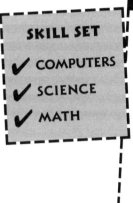

SKILL SET

✔ COMPUTERS

✔ SCIENCE

✔ MATH

SHORTCUTS

GO visit the Unix Sysadm Resources website (http://www.stokely.com/stokely/unix.sysadm.resources/index.html). It gets a little complicated in places, but explore the site and see what you can find.

READ *Boardwatch*, the magazine of the on-line industry. You can find it in many libraries and bookstores.

TRY installing a modem or Internet-connection software on a computer. Read the instructions very carefully.

WHAT IS AN INTERNET SYSTEMS ADMINISTRATOR?

The Internet is the new Wild West, and the systems administrators are the new sheriffs. Sure, they have a lot of technical problems to deal with, but many of the problems are more human in nature: people trying to break into computers or hiding illegally obtained software.

An Internet service provider (ISP) is a company that sells access to the Internet. America Online and CompuServe are large ISPs, but there are many thousands of small ISPs too. ISPs range from companies with just one or two employees, to huge national or international companies with thousands of employees. The systems administrator's job is to keep the ISP's computers running and to make sure that the company's customers are able to connect to the Internet.

The systems administrator is therefore responsible for many things. The most important responsibility is keeping the

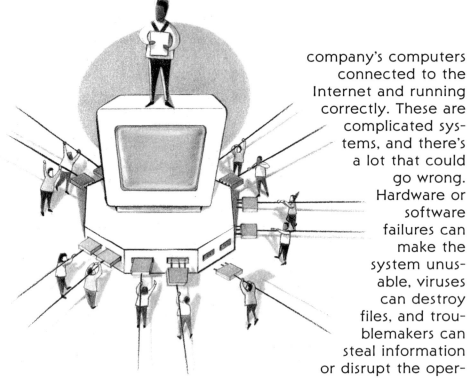

company's computers connected to the Internet and running correctly. These are complicated systems, and there's a lot that could go wrong. Hardware or software failures can make the system unusable, viruses can destroy files, and troublemakers can steal information or disrupt the operations. These are all concerns of the systems administrator.

The systems administrator is also responsible for upgrading equipment and for installing new equipment as the company grows. It doesn't take long for computers and modems to become out of date in this business. It seems as through everybody in the entire industry replaces most of their modems every 18 months or so.

There's more too. The systems administrator may have to help customers with their software configuration problems, especially if he or she is working for a small service provider (larger companies have technical-support departments that handle this sort of thing). While much better now than just two or three years ago, Internet-connection software is still tricky to configure in many cases, and in small companies the administrator may spend a lot of time on the phone or perhaps even making "house calls" to help customers get everything set up properly. The administrator may also have to help large business customers set up their networks and perhaps provide training as well.

One of the most exciting parts of the job is battling the computer break-ins. A computer cracker is someone who tries to break into other people's computers by exploiting the network link with the outside world. Someone sitting at a computer connected to the Internet in Germany, for example, can attempt to break into another Internet-connected computer in Mexico. A prime target is the Internet service provider's system. In many cases, crackers are just out to see how far they can get, just for fun. In some cases, they are carrying out malicious acts, intentionally damaging systems. And in other cases, they're using ISP systems as "way stations," places to store stolen software for a short time.

A skilled systems administrator can watch for break-ins and take steps to thwart the attacker's actions. The administrator may even be able to track down where the cracker is operating and then contact the administrator of the system being used by the cracker. Sometimes, a cat and mouse game begins as the administrator searches for the cracker and works to have the cracker thrown off the system. The cracker may then find another system and return, breaking in again. It's a battle that's never quite won. The systems administrator is the sheriff of his or her system, and the sheriffs often work together—forming a posse, almost—to fight the bad guys on the Internet.

TRY IT OUT

FIND A NETWORK

You'll probably find it difficult to get your hands on the expensive equipment that Internet service providers use, but there are similarities between networks of all kinds. Does your school computer lab have a network? It probably has Internet access. Try to find out about all the connections.

Track down the school systems administrator or the computer teacher, and ask if you can spend some time watching him or her working on the network—installing network connections or modems, for instance, or configuring the network software.

It's quite complicated stuff, but if you ask lots of questions, you may be able to pick up some of the jargon and basic networking concepts.

READ A CYBERADVENTURE

There are a number of good books about hackers and crackers. (A hacker is someone who loves fooling around with computers, seeing what he or she can get the computers to do. A cracker is someone who breaks into computer systems, often intending to steal data or damage the system. The media often confuse these two terms, so the term *hacker* is often used when *cracker* is more appropriate.) Chasing crackers is not the only responsibility of the systems administrator, but it is one of the most fun. The following books will give you a feel for life on the network.

Hafner, Katie, and John Markoff. *Cyberpunk: Outlaws and Hackers on the Computer Frontier.* New York: Touchstone, 1995.

Levy, Steven. *Hackers: Heroes of the Computer Revolution.* New York: Delta, 1994.

Shimomura, Tsutomu, and John Markoff. *Takedown: The Pursuit and Capture of Kevin Mitnick, America's Most Wanted Computer Outlaw—By the Man Who Did It.* New York: Hyperion, 1996.

Sterling, Bruce. *The Hacker Crackdown: Law and Disorder on the Electronic Frontier.* New York: Bantam, 1993.

LEARN TO PROGRAM

Programming is an essential skill for a systems administrator. It's not a full-time task, so administrators tend not to be the world's best programmers, but they do experiment with programming now and again, in particular with relatively simple scripting languages such as Perl.

Ask your computer teacher for help with a scripting language. You might try simple JavaScript; all you need is a copy of Netscape Navigator or Internet Explorer and a simple book on JavaScript, such as co-author Peter Kent's *Official Netscape JavaScript 1.2* (Phoenix: Ventana, 1997). You might also try creating macros in a word processor such as Word for Windows; these are simple scripts and all you need is the word processor and a good book. Also, take a look at the Artificial Intelligence Scientist and Computer Game Design chapters for information on Lingo, a kid's programming language.

CHECK IT OUT

North American Internet Service Providers' Association (naISPa)
E-mail: naispa-l@naispa.org
Web: http://www.naispa.org/

Systems Administrators Guild (SAGE)
USENIX Association
2560 Ninth Street, Suite 215
Berkeley, California 94710
E-mail: office@usenix.org
Web: http://www.usenix.org/sage

GET ACQUAINTED

Rachel Drummond, Internet Systems Administrator

CAREER PATH

CHILDHOOD ASPIRATION: To be a marine biologist, firefighter, welder, or physicist. She never realized that anyone could use computers to make a living.

FIRST JOB: Receptionist at Expert Internet Service.

CURRENT JOB: Systems administrator at Expert Internet Service.

WORKING HER WAY UP THE LADDER

Rachel Drummond has loved computers for a long time. She first programmed her Atari 800 when she was 10, making it play violin music. She'd always hoped her parents would buy her a bigger, more powerful computer, but she probably lost that chance when she set the Atari to play a mind-numbing music loop and turned the volume up full blast for hours on end.

She was 22 before she got her next computer, which she used to connect to GEnie, an on-line service. Drummond was launching a short-story magazine named *Sequitur* and started a discussion group on GEnie in order to promote the magazine.

While in high school, Drummond attended classes in the school district's Career Enrichment Center, where they offered bricklaying classes, beautician classes, and computer classes. The center had a big mainframe computer, and Drummond learned how to program in Assembly, BASIC, and FORTRAN.

HOOKED ON THE INTERNET

After college, where she studied engineering and physics, she found herself unemployed and looking for a job, but she stayed connected to the Internet for hours at a time, reading news group messages and using role-playing games such as MUDs (Multi-User Dungeons) and MUSHes (Multi-User Shared Hallucinations). In those days, 1994, Internet access was expensive, and Drummond couldn't afford to pay the eight hours she was on-line each day. So, she called her Internet service provider and offered to trade some part-time work in return for on-line time. She started working at Expert Internet Service as the receptionist.

While working as the receptionist, she discovered main pages. These are the on-line documents that explain UNIX programs, and Drummond began reading all she could find. The more she read, the more she learned. Of course, as she was receptionist, she often answered calls from customers who had problems. Since her boss couldn't keep up with all the calls, Drummond started tackling some of them herself.

Soon her boss realized that she knew more about some subjects than he did, and he would pass questions on to her. Eventually he realized that she could answer most customer questions better than he could, so he gave her the systems administrator job.

THE THRILL OF THE CHASE

Drummond loves keeping up on the technology because there's so much to learn. She especially loves the constant variety. She also enjoys having to solve the problems that occur when the equipment is malfunctioning. But the part of the job she loves most is chasing people!

She chases spammers (people sending huge amounts of unwanted e-mail across the Internet) and gets their Internet accounts closed, and she chases people who abuse the Expert Internet Service computer system. "I feel like some-one's broken into my house!" she says. "I get furious, very protective, and I'm not going to let them get away with it."

Drummond is partly responsible for the very first prosecution of an Internet software pirate. The cracker broke into the Expert Internet Service system, created hidden directories, and then stored over 600 MB of "cracked" software (that is, computer programs that have been modified so that they can be used without a registration number). This is a common trick used by software pirates. They store the files on a computer that they've broken into—hoping that the administrator hasn't noticed—and then tell other people that they can go to the site to download the software. Only this time, this system administrator *did* notice.

In conjunction with the Software Publishers Association, Drummond began tracking the cracker's actions. She was able to track him back to his Internet access point, and eventually he was caught by the police in San Francisco. Unfortunately, he jumped bail and traveled up and down the West coast before being caught again in Seattle.

In another case, Drummond assisted the North Carolina Bureau of Investigations in tracking down a cracker—and was offered a job in return. For now, though, she's happy where she is.

Multimedia Developer

SHORTCUTS

SKILL SET

✔ ART

✔ WRITING

✔ COMPUTERS

GO visit a computer store that has demo software running and spend time playing with the best multimedia programs they have available.

READ *Multimedia and CD-ROMs for Dummies* by Andy Rathbone (Indianapolis: IDG, 1997).

TRY using all the graphics and animation software you can find at school, home, or the library.

WHAT IS A MULTIMEDIA DEVELOPER?

You've seen multimedia in computer games, CD encyclopedias and books, and on the World Wide Web. It involves a creative blend of graphics, animation, video, graphics, and text to provide information and entertainment in an interactive computer environment. Good multimedia is very expensive and complicated to create, so it takes a team of people to do all the many required tasks.

Producing a multimedia product is comparable to making a movie. In the film business, you have actors, artists, camera operators, makeup people, and directors. Multimedia developers are the directors of the multimedia business. They steer the multimedia project in the right direction, ensuring that everyone involved is moving toward the same goal.

Who else is involved in a multimedia project? That depends on what's going into the project. Almost all multimedia projects have artists and writers, the people who create the pictures and text. They also have programmers, who take all the words and pictures and put them into the multimedia program. The artists may also be involved in creating animation, although some projects require an animation specialist. Voice "talent" (actors who provide vocals for the project) may be required; in many small multimedia projects, however, the voices are provided by the artists, writers, developers, and other staff. More sophisticated projects involve professional actors as well.

The multimedia developer runs the show and plans the overall project. Two tasks are at the heart of the developer's job: designing the look and feel of the product and managing the overall project. Although the developer may also be part of the creative team, he or she manages the project by delegating tasks, scheduling goals, and making sure that these goals are met.

Although computer multimedia has been around quite awhile, it was more promise than reality, more hype than

truth. You've probably noticed that many multimedia programs are a real disappointment. They look fantastic on the box, but when you actually install and run the programs, you find that they're slow and boring. The major reason behind this is that the average computer is not powerful enough to handle all the "bells and whistles" of a full-fledged multimedia program. The hardware is just beginning to catch up with the software, so only recently have multimedia developers been able to turn their imaginations into some really spectacular programs, and the best is yet to come.

Hardware isn't the only thing lagging behind developments in multimedia. Education is too. There are some college courses on multimedia, but they're still a bit weak and often don't teach the skills that the developer really needs.

If you are interested in a career in this field, you can begin by learning as much as you can about graphics, animation, audio software, and even some basic programming. By the time you're ready to enter the profession, both the hardware and the educational opportunities should be available to prepare you to create some impressive multimedia programs.

TRY IT OUT

GET INTERACTIVE

One of the best ways to learn about multimedia is to experiment with a variety of graphics and animation programs. There are many of these around, but here are two that you might want to investigate.

- ☼ **Corel Printhouse Magic and Corel Galleria Magic.** Together, these programs provide the tools you need to produce everything from a poster to an interactive video presentation. The programs include 200,000 samples of clip art, fonts, and video sound clips. Call 800-772-6735 for information or visit Corel's website at http:/www.custserv@corel.ca.

☀ **Microsoft Publisher**. This program provides easy-to-use templates for integrating text and graphics into some great-looking publications. For information call Microsoft at 800-426-9400 or visit its website at http://www.microsoft.com.

One word of advice. Multimedia programs vary greatly in their power, usability, and cost. To find one that fits your computer skills and budget, talk with a knowledgeable sales-person at your local computer store or call 800-EGGHEAD for ideas.

SPEND TIME ON THE WEB

You probably won't be surprised to hear that there's plenty of information about multimedia on the World Wide Web. Search for the word *multimedia* through any major search engine, and you'll come up with hundreds of sites to visit.

Or you could go directly to the following sites, which list useful places to visit.

☀ Index to Multimedia Information Sources at http://viswiz.gmd.de/MultimediaInfo/ offers a huge list of multimedia related sites, sorted into categories.
☀ Media WorldWide at http://www.wwug.com offers articles and discussion groups about multimedia.

Two other sites to visit include the World Wide Web multimedia magazines *Multimedia Café* (http://www.worldvillage.com/cafe/) and *ITP Review* (http://www.itp.tsoa.nyu.edu/~review/).

Also, check out these two magazines on-line. If you like them, save up for your own subscription.

Music and Computers
P.O. Box 56220
Boulder, Colorado 80322-6220
http://www.music-and-computers.com

Electronic Musician
P.O. Box 41525
Nashville, Tennessee 37204-9829
http://www.emusician.com/

GO BEHIND THE SCENES

One book in particular provides an imaginative and informative look at the process of producing multimedia programs. *Multimedia: The Complete Guide* (New York: DK Publishing, 1996) includes 500 photographs and a step-by-step guide to how multimedia video, graphics, animation, and sound are made.

GO TO CYBER SCHOOL

If you have access to America Online, you have access to a free multimedia education. Start at the Channels directory and choose the Computing site. From there, it's a click on "on-line classroom" and another click on "multimedia," and you'll find all kinds of how-tos and tutorials on the best tools in the industry.

CHECK IT OUT

Association for Multimedia Communications (AMC)
P.O. Box 10645
Chicago, Illinois 60610
E-mail: amc@amcomm.org
Web: http://www.amcomm.org/

National Multimedia Association of America (NMAA)
4920 Niagara Road, Third Floor
College Park, Maryland 20740
Phone: 800-819-1335
E-mail: info@nmaa.org
Web: Use a browser to search for the NMAA website.

GET ACQUAINTED

Kurt Matthies, Multimedia Developer

CAREER PATH

CHILDHOOD ASPIRATION: To be a rock'n'roll star.

FIRST JOB: Kidney dialysis technician.

CURRENT JOB: President of Mesa Interactive.

FROM ROCK'N'ROLL TO ENGINEERING

Kurt Matthies comes from a family of musicians, and for a while he wanted to be a professional rock'n'roll musician himself. At the age of 17, however, he realized he wasn't good enough to be truly successful. Having seen firsthand how musicians live if they don't manage to make it to the top, he decided to take another path.

He moved from his home in New Jersey to Los Angeles, where he got a steady job as a dialysis technician in a clinic. After working in the clinic for five years, he decided to go to college to earn an engineering degree and attended San Francisco State University. That's where he first began working with computers.

COMPUTER CAREER #1

Matthies taught himself how to program in UNIX and discovered that you have to be good at teaching yourself in this business. Once he could program, he got a job as a UNIX programmer. After a couple of years of programming, he realized that he'd much rather *talk* about programming than actually do it, so he found a job with a training company

61

teaching subjects such as UNIX basics, UNIX architecture, and system administration. This job took him all over the world to interesting places such as Australia, Japan, Singapore, Germany, Finland, and Hong Kong.

Eventually he tired of all the travel and decided that he had to do something new.

COMPUTER CAREER #2

This was the beginning of the PC revolution, when small, less expensive computers were finally available to ordinary people. Again Matthies set about teaching himself something new; this time he put together a PC clone and taught himself Pascal, another common programming language. This lead to another foray into the world of computer programming, writing software for a spell checker, a credit-card encryption system, and an information system used in Bradley Fighting Vehicles.

COMPUTER CAREER #3

Next Matthies found the Macintosh and fell in love with it. He was intrigued with the way you could mix text and graphics, so he set about learning to write programs for the Macintosh. These were the early days of the Macintosh, so few people knew much about them. Matthies found himself in a position to lead the way. He starting writing a regular programming column in *Mac User*. Later he wrote a book about programming on the Mac, published by Microsoft Press.

It was about this time that an editor showed Matthies a copy of Microsoft Multimedia Viewer—and his next career began.

MULTIMEDIA BEGINNINGS

Microsoft Multimedia Viewer was an early multimedia authoring and hypertext program. Hypertext is the system that links electronic pages, allowing you to click on a word in one page and up pops related or corresponding text from another page. Matthies thought this was fantastic, and he convinced a major computer mouse company—Logitech—to allow him to create an on-line tutorial for one of its products. He knew next to nothing about Multimedia Viewer when he began, but by the time he'd finished, he knew more about it than virtually anyone.

Since then Matthies has been running his own multimedia business, Mesa Interactive. Initially the company created Windows Help files, hypertext systems that are closely related to Microsoft Multimedia Viewer and that may contain some multimedia components. As the business grew, it developed more complicated and exciting multimedia projects.

THE GOOD AND THE BAD

One of the difficult things about the multimedia business is that it's hard to keep up with the technology; the tools and technologies are constantly changing. But that's also one of the exciting things; there's always something new to learn. "Multimedia is a fantastic mix of jobs," says Matthies. "Art, words, programming, and you get to work with some really creative people."

On-Line Researcher

SHORTCUTS

SKILL SET

✔ COMPUTERS

✔ BUSINESS

✔ ADVENTURE

GO volunteer at your public or school library. Learn as much as possible about how the librarians find the answers to people's questions.

READ *The Information Broker's Handbook* by Sue Rugge and Alfred Glossbrenner (New York: McGraw-Hill, 1997).

TRY finding out on the Net the origin and meaning of your name.

WHAT IS AN ON-LINE RESEARCHER?

An on-line researcher is someone who looks for answers to questions. Many different types of companies employ researchers to find the information they need to do business. Law firms, for example, need to research legal precedent, meaning they need to find earlier legal cases that have a bearing on cases the firm is currently handling. Brokerage companies research investments, and companies that design high-tech products research competing products. Also drug companies look for research that relates to new drugs they are developing. Finding answers to questions such as these can be challenging.

Researchers look for the answers in many different places. Among them are special databases—both those that are stored on compact disks and those that are available on-line. These databases are not the kind that just anyone can find on the Internet. Instead, they tend to be pay-as-you-search business databases such as Dialog, Lexis-Nexis, and Dow Jones. These on-line databases, systems that have huge quantities of valuable business information, have been around for years. Lexis-Nexis claims that it adds almost 10 million documents each week.

With hundreds of millions of documents stored in databases around the world, how is it possible to find just the one you need? A well-trained and competent researcher knows where to look for the information or, at least, how to figure out where to look. It's not just a matter of typing in a few key words into a search program and clicking a button. The researcher must understand what sort of information is likely to be found in which database. And even then, researching a single question may be a long, drawn-out process, with each little piece of information leading to another. Research is often like solving a mystery: You follow all the clues you can find and stay in hot pursuit of the ultimate answer.

In addition to using high-tech resources such as these databases, most researchers become exceptionally good at tracking down information on the Internet as well as in more traditional formats such as microfiche or paper directories.

Most researchers work for large companies, often in corporate libraries. But there's great potential in this career for starting your own business. A research firm can be set up with a relatively small investment. Many experienced researchers quit their jobs and go into business for themselves.

If you think you might be interested in a career as an on-line researcher, consider getting a degree in library science as a starting point. Although a degree isn't essential, it's certainly very helpful. A liberal-arts education can be very useful too. For instance, an English degree with lots of electives provides a broad-based education. While many researchers have a specialty—medicine or business, for example—a very broad range of knowledge helps the researcher find connections in information.

As a student, you may have already had a chance to test your research abilities while working on a term paper or class project. If you enjoyed the process of tracking down information and organizing it for a presentation, you'll want to consider the possibility of making this part of your future career.

TRY IT OUT

EXPERIMENT ON THE INTERNET

Although on-line researchers do most of their research in databases that charge a fee for access, the Internet provides lots of "toys" for you to experiment with. There are hundreds of search engines on the Internet, each working a little differently from the others. Experiment with a few of these search engines; in Netscape Navigator or Internet Explorer, click the search button to see a list of popular search engines, or go to one of these URLs:

- **Yahoo!** at http://www.yahoo.com/
- **AltaVista** at http://www.altavista.digital.com/
- **Excite** at http://www.excite.com/
- **Infoseek** at http://www.infoseek.com/

Begin by reading the Help information at each site, and learn how to create a search (you'll notice that each system is slightly different). Start with simple searches; then see how these search engines allow you to do more complicated searches. Also read how these search systems catalog and store different types of information; for example, AltaVista indexes entire pages and as many websites as it can reach, while Yahoo! creates a short entry for the websites that its staff has hand-selected to place in the database. Search for information about a class project you're working on, or see if you can answer these questions:

Where do tree kangaroos live?
Who is Edward Tufte?
What does the U.S. Airforce's Blackbird look like?
What is the best way to grow roses?

LEARN BOOLEAN LOGIC

Ask your math or computer teacher about Boolean logic. This is the system used by most on-line databases to allow people to mix search terms. For instance, you can tell a database that you want to find information about Disneyland and Mickey Mouse, but not Goofy. A search like that could be presented in this manner: Disneyland AND Mickey Mouse NOT Goofy. The search engine would only find articles that include information about Disneyland *and* Mickey Mouse; articles that contain information on Goofy *but not* Mickey Mouse would be ignored, as would any article that includes information about Goofy *and* Mickey Mouse. Once you understand Boolean logic—and it's really not terribly complicated—you'll understand the basics of database searching.

CLIMB YOUR FAMILY TREE

Here's a project to put your research skills to the test and to put you in touch with your family roots. Go back in time and find out all you can about your ancestors. Programs like Broderbund's Family Tree Maker make it challenging enough to be interesting but easy enough to be fun. This program comes with 4 CDs of data, plus a special Internet search tool that can be used to find even the most elusive skeletons in your family's closet.

For information about Broderbund's Family Tree Maker, visit your local computer software store or write to Broderbund at 500 Redwood Boulevard, Novato, California 94948.

CHECK IT OUT

American Society for Information Science
8720 Georgia Avenue, Suite 501
Silver Spring, Maryland 20910
E-mail: asis@asis.org
Web: http://www.asis.org/

Association of Independent Information Professionals
234 West Delaware Avenue
Pennington, New Jersey 08534
E-mail: aiipinfo@aiip.org
Web: http://www.aiip.org

GET ACQUAINTED

Susan Krauss, On-Line Researcher

CAREER PATH

CHILDHOOD ASPIRATION: To be a teacher.

FIRST JOB: Clerical work in the legal department of a New York advertising firm.

CURRENT JOB: President of Krauss Research.

DISCOVERING RESEARCH

Susan Krauss graduated with a degree in English and communications from the University of Michigan, completely unaware of the existence of her future career. Unsure of what to do—she was thinking about pursuing a law degree—Krauss took a job in the legal department of a New York advertising company. One day she was sent to the corporate library and realized that it would be a great place to work.

Krauss had always been interested in research. Even as a kid she had researched subjects, although she didn't really think of it that way. She had kept newspaper clippings on subjects that interested her—folk music and the Vietnam War, for instance—and loved digging up new information. Also while at college, as part of a work-study program, she had participated in a research project for a local public radio station, building a database of information about the music on the station's old records. "It's a wonder nobody ever told me I should be doing this for a career," Krauss said. "I had no idea I could get paid to do research!"

A quick word with the advertising company's personnel department, letting them know that she'd love to work in the library, was all it took. The very next day she had her new job—corporate librarian—and the beginning of a new career.

BACK TO SCHOOL

Having discovered the career she'd always wanted, she decided to earn a degree in library science. Although the degree wasn't absolutely necessary, Krauss found that it taught her some great research skills.

To balance work and school more easily, she had to take a less demanding job, working for a nonprofit organization. After graduating and with more time to devote to her job, she moved to an accounting firm and got a large raise. A few years later, she started her own business, Krauss Research.

NO SUCH THING AS A FREE LUNCH

No career is without problem, and as much as Krauss loves research, there are days when it can be frustrating. "People don't realize how much work is involved in research; they think answers should be immediately accessible, and cheap too." The growth of the Internet has led many people to assume this.

The truth is that information is often hard to find. "Sometimes there simply *isn't* an answer, and people don't understand why they should have to pay. But they're paying for the research, not the answer," notes Krauss.

Krauss recommends that potential researchers take classes that will give them a chance to hone their research skills. She says there's one thing you really don't need—a good memory. "I have a terrible memory, but being a researcher is not about remembering facts. It's about knowing how to find the answers you're looking for."

Repair Technician

SHORTCUTS

SKILL SET

✔ COMPUTERS

✔ SCIENCE

✔ BUSINESS

GO to your local computer store to ask if you can visit the repair technicians "behind the scenes." Watch them at work for a little while and ask what they're doing.

READ Building Your Own PC by Arnie Lee (Grand Rapids, Mich.: Abacus, 1997).

TRY installing a software program on a computer at school or at home. Follow the instructions very carefully.

WHAT IS A REPAIR TECHNICIAN?

You may have noticed by now that computers require lots of attention and maintenance. There always seems to be something going wrong with them: perhaps the modem you installed a few weeks ago isn't working properly, or you installed one program and now another has stopped working. Computers are very complicated, which is good news for computer repair technicians. There are plenty of problems to fix! You might think of the repair technicians as the plumbers of the computer world. Just as when the water pipes burst, when a computer malfunctions, most people don't know what to do and must rely on the expertise of a professional who does. And, just as with plumbers, people pay their computer repair technicians a lot for their services and expertise.

The first part of any repair job requires troubleshooting or figuring out what's wrong. A computer problem can be caused by either hardware or software. A repair technician may have to use special programs to restore lost data or may have to replace a malfunctioning part. Other frequent software problems include cleaning up a computer's configuration settings to get things to run properly. And some

customers even pay to have software installed, to make sure it's done right.

Hardware problems can be just as varied. Hard disks are sometimes physically damaged by an electrical surge or by being dropped, and a repair technician will try to retrieve the data left on the disk. Computer screens often stop working, power supplies fail, or RAM (random access memory) sometimes acts up. All these problems can be fixed by the repair technician.

There's no established educational route for this job. There is a variety of certification programs created by some of the large software companies, such as Microsoft and Novell. A number of colleges have courses on computer repair. Far more important than a particular body of knowledge is a particular aptitude. You need to be persistent, and a good problem-solver who can find solutions by drawing on experience as well as by trial and error. Because there's such a wide range of hardware and software products, you can never learn everything. What you can do, however, is to get a feel for problems and what might be causing them.

If you're interested in a career as a computer technician, take some high school electronics classes. While in high school, you might also try to get a part-time job working in a computer retail store; what you'll learn about computer products and jargon will help tremendously. You might also take community college courses on computer repair and maintenance.

Once you've learned the ropes, you'll find plenty of opportunity awaiting a skilled repair technician in computer stores, in electronic repair shops, or as an independent businessperson.

TRY IT OUT

PLAY WITH A VOLTMETER

A basic tool of the repair technician is the voltmeter. A voltmeter is used to check voltages and other electrical characteristics such as circuit continuity (that is, to see if an electrical circuit is broken or is continuous). Someone at your school almost certainly has one; ask the science teacher.

Try a few things. Check the voltage on small batteries, C- or D-size batteries for instance. And see how the device can check circuit continuity by touching the contacts on the ends of a single wire. Try other substances to see if an electrical charge can flow through them; touch each side of a coin, different sides of a computer case, different sides of a filing cabinet, and so on. Checking for circuit continuity is an important technique for the repair technician, because broken circuits mean electrical signals no longer get through.

TAKE A PEEK

Ask the computer teacher or your parent if you can take a look inside a computer. Make sure that the computer is unplugged and that an adult is supervising. Try to identify all the different components. Use the computer manual to double-check your guesses.

Start by identifying the components that can be accessed from the outside: the floppy and CD drives and the printer, serial, and telephone line ports at the back. Look for the hard drives too. See how these components are connected to the motherboard, the large computer board inside the computer. You should be able to see the power supply, a big box tucked away in one corner of the computer case.

Then try to identify the other components on the board: the memory chips, the processor, the small battery that keeps the computer's clock going, and the little jumper switches that are used to configure the computer's settings. Also try to identify any boards that are plugged into the motherboard: the modem, floppy drive controller, SCSI card, and so on.

Be careful not to touch anything! Static electricity from your fingers can damage sensitive electronic components.

BUILD A BETTER COMPUTER

For the truly adventurous, there's always the option of building your own computer. You can find all the parts you'll need at a well-stocked computer store, or check your local phone directory for used computer stores or stores that specialize in customized computers. Depending on the configuration, you can build your own computer for as little as $200 (or as much as $4,000 to $5,000). Before you start buying parts, figure out what you want in terms of memory, software, and other options. Make a list and check off each item as you find it. Lee Arnie's *Building Your Own PC* (Grand Rapids, Mich.: Abacus, 1997) will provide inspiration and instructions during the project.

CHECK IT OUT

Electronics Technicians Association–International, Inc.
602 North Jackson
Greencastle, Indiana 46135
E-mail: eta@indy.tdsnet.com
Web: http://www.eta-sda.com/

International Society of Certified Electronics Technicians (ISCET)
2708 West Berry Street, Suite 3
Fort Worth, Texas 76109
E-mail: iscetAB@aol.com
Web: http://www.iscet.org/

GET ACQUAINTED

Mike Little, Repair Technician

CAREER PATH

CHILDHOOD ASPIRATION: To do anything involved with new technologies.

FIRST JOB: Computer programmer.

CURRENT JOB: Owner of Techs-On-Call.

THANKS, RADIO SHACK!

When personal computers first arrived on the scene, in the late 1970s, Mike Little found them fascinating. He also found them expensive. In those days the schools didn't have computers, but Radio Shack did. In fact, Radio Shack was really the only place at the time where you could find computers that were accessible to kids. So Little would spend as much time as he could playing with the computers in his local mall's Radio Shack. He could sometimes stay as long as two hours before the staff would throw him out (which was occasionally long enough to create password programs to lock the staff out of their own computers!).

Little taught himself BASIC programming in Radio Shack, working with primitive personal computers such as Radio Shack's TRS-80. He just sat down, read the manuals, and tried out everything he learned.

COLLEGE ON THE BEACH

When he was 19, Little went to Pepperdine University in Malibu, California, just a couple of blocks from the beach. There he studied computer science and learned more about programming. When he finished college, he took a job as a programmer with a company creating a spreadsheet program. He soon discovered that even programmers have to experiment with hardware. The company he worked for seemed to run into more hardware problems than software problems, so Little soon learned the skills needed to keep computers running.

Little left this job after about a year and decided to take it easy for a while. He took on mainly part-time jobs, but he kept running into people who needed computers fixed, networks set up, or software installed. He found himself spending more and more time fixing things. No longer was he just doing a job long enough to make money to survive or to go on vacation; there was so much work finding him that it was turning into a full-time occupation.

TECHS-ON-CALL IS BORN

"No matter where I went or what I was doing, I ended up fixing people's computers," says Little. "'Hey I've got this computer problem,' people would say to me at parties. 'What do I do?' It was getting ridiculous, so I decided it was time to get serious."

In 1993 he got a business license and started Techs-On-Call. Since then his business has doubled each year. "I wake up every day thanking Bill Gates," he says. "He keeps me in business." Techs-On-Call now employs four people. They fix computers, of course, but they also install networks and cabling, install software and fix software problems, and, just recently, have got into the business of setting up World Wide Web pages.

Two things make Little's business stand out in the world of computer repair. First, his company makes "house calls." Most companies make the customer bring the computer to them, but Little's company brings the tech to the computer—a very convenient service for many busy people.

Also, Little's employees are trained to be responsive on the human level, a trait that's often missing in computer experts. His technicians talk to the clients, explaining what they are doing and why, and exactly how much it will cost. "When people call you with computer problems, they're frantic. They're losing time or maybe even data," Little says. "You have to have an extraordinary amount of patience with them, to talk with them and tell them just what has to be done to fix their problems."

Software Entrepreneur

SHORTCUTS

SKILL SET

✔ COMPUTERS

✔ BUSINESS

✔ TALKING

GO listen in on Internet news groups related to shareware, such as alt.comp.shareware and alt.comp.shareware.authors. Eventually jump in and ask how people got started in the business. You're bound to get some interesting answers!

READ *How I Sold a Million Copies of My Software and How You Can Too* by Herbert R. Kraft (Holbrook, Mass.: Adams Media, 1997).

TRY downloading a shareware program. These programs are created by software entrepreneurs.

WHAT IS A SOFTWARE ENTREPRENEUR?

A software entrepreneur is someone in the business of developing and selling his or her own software. The great thing about this business is that it's still possible for a single person to come up with a good idea, write a program, and sell it.

You probably already know of at least one software entrepreneur: Bill Gates, the founder of Microsoft. But there are thousands more, from people who've made a comfortable living selling their own software to people who've become multimillionaires. In fact we've already highlighted other entrepreneurs in this book: Will Wright (the cofounder of Maxis—see Computer Game Design) and Victor Kushdilian (owner of SportsWare—see Computer Programmer).

In the early days of the personal compucter, it was relatively easy for a software entrepreneur to get started. There were so few people involved at the beginning that someone who had a good idea and was prepared to work hard could create one of the first programs of a particular type, getting a head start on an entire area of programming. Will Wright, for instance, bought the Commodore 64 computer as soon as it came out, shut himself in his room, and wrote what would be the first game for that computer.

Things have changed. Now there are many thousands of software companies producing programs for PCs. But that doesn't mean there isn't room for an individual programmer to set up business. The key today is to come up with an idea for a program that hasn't been written or to make dramatic improvements in a program that already exists. With more people using computers, there's plenty of room for all sorts of programs. For example when only a small number of people had computers, there wasn't much of a market for a program that would help people keep records about their body-building workouts. These days, however, there are several bodybuilding programs on the market. Is there a market for software to help people keep records of the dog shows they attend? For software that provides information for amateur sailors, such

as tide tables and sunset times? For programs that help hobbyists with building and launching their model rockets? Maybe. Maybe not. The secret to a successful software entrepreneurship is to find a niche that nobody else has discovered and write a program that people will want to buy.

Good programming skills are, of course, essential to success in the software business. But as an entrepreneur, strong business and communication skills are just as important. You can write the best program in the world, but if you don't know how to promote it, you'll never sell it.

Many entrepreneurs begin distributing their software as shareware; they give away the programs on the Internet and on-line services. If users like the software, they can register to get a manual, a more advanced version of the program, free upgrades, and so on. Shareware provides a way for a talented programmer to get into the business with almost no initial cost—beyond the time it takes to develop the program, of course.

TRY IT OUT

GET THE IDEA HABIT

Every brilliant innovation starts with a single idea. Make sure you are ready to capture your best thoughts by keeping an idea notebook. Every time you have an idea about a new twist on a computer program, jot it down. Don't worry if at first you don't come up with ideas. Once you've "programmed" your mind to look for ideas, it will discover them even when you're not consciously looking for them. Keep the book handy because you never know when the best ideas might hit—while cleaning up in the kitchen, traveling on the school bus, or watching a movie.

Consider ways to link computer programs with specific jobs, hobbies, or tasks. Think about how programs are used: They store information, make calculations, "create" things (pictures, sounds, words), and so on. Look for ideas in which these basic procedures can be applied in some new way.

DATABASE DISCOVERY

A very quick way to get into the software business is by creating a specialized database program, a program that is used to store information for a particular purpose. In fact, many programs have as their primary purpose the storage of data. For instance, e-mail programs and computer phone books are basically database programs used to store e-mail messages and information about people.

Your school probably has several database programs available, from the quite simple—Microsoft Works, for instance—to the quite complicated, such as Microsoft Access and Claris FileMaker Pro. Learn how to use these programs.

After you've gotten familiar with those, create your own database. Make it useful and fun. Perhaps you could design something to keep track of homework assignments or the school's sports statistics.

FREE FOR THE TAKING

Spend some time looking at the thousands of shareware programs available. The great thing about shareware is that you can download these programs and use them to get an idea about what other people are doing. Then you need to pay a registration fee only if you decide to continue using the program.

You'll find shareware areas in all the large on-line services. You can also use these great shareware sites on the web.

- **Info-Mac HyperArchive** (http://www.pht.com/info-mac/)
- **Jumbo!** (http://www.jumbo.com/)
- **Shareware.com** (http://www.shareware.com/)
- **Tucows** (http://www.tucows.com/)
- **Ultimate Macintosh Site** (http://www.flashpaper.com/~mac/)
- **University of Texas Mac Archive** (http://wwwhost.ots.utexas.edu/mac/main.html)
- **Windows95.com** (http://www.infiles.com/)
- **Winsite** (http://www.winsite.com/)

CHECK IT OUT

Association of Shareware Professionals (ASP)
Software Co-Op
5437 Honey Manor Drive
Indianapolis, Indiana 46221
E-mail: president@asp-shareware.org
Web: http://www.asp-shareware.org/

Shareware Author Network
Biondo Software
P.O. Box 212
Morton Grove, Illinois 60053
E-mail: info@bsoftware.com
Web: http://www.bsoftware.com/snetwork.htm

GET ACQUAINTED

Phil Bair, Software
Entrepreneur

CAREER PATH

CHILDHOOD ASPIRATION: To be an astronaut.

FIRST JOB: Gas station attendant, changing oil and fixing flat tires.

CURRENT JOB: Software engineer and owner of AirLogic, a software development company.

THE LOGICAL CONNECTION

When Phil Bair graduated from high school, he wasn't sure what he wanted to do. He went to an adult friend (who also happened to be his boss); his friend suggested that a career in computers might be a good fit with Bair's sharp logic skills.

Bair took his advice and signed up for computer classes at a vocational/technical school.

The program provided a good foundation of computer skills, and once Bair learned the basics, he was off and running, ready to learn new things on his own. The trade-off for choosing a highly specialized training program over a traditional college program was that he missed out on getting a well-rounded education.

HIGH-TECH BABY-SITTER

Bair went to school during the day and worked as a computer operator in a large hospital at night. He worked the graveyard shift from 11:00 P.M. to 8:00 A.M., and he describes his chief responsibility as being a high-tech "baby-sitter." While most people slept, Bair kept the hospital's mainframe computer on track and ran a huge assortment of reports. It was a good opportunity to see firsthand how a large organization uses information.

PROGRAMMER FOR HIRE

Immediately after graduating, Bair was offered his first programming job with a big farmer's co-op. He was responsible for helping develop a data-entry program, for training new computer operators, and for providing ongoing technical support to the company's computer users.

It was here that Bair honed two important skills. First, he had the chance to learn how to solve problems with computers. Second, he discovered a natural talent for helping other people understand how to use computers. As he continued to advance in his career, these two elements came into play again and again.

WILD BLUE YONDER

While Bair's early experience centered on hospitals and health care organizations, he eventually started working in the airline industry. There, another friend's advice helped convince Bair to form his own company. The friend said that

Bair was an above-average computer programmer and should be doing more with his skills.

The friend got a chance to put some action behind his words when a London-based company introduced new technology that could automate a number of routine airline tasks. The only problem was that there was no software available to allow airlines to take advantage of the new technology. He encouraged Bair to write a program, and the two men formed a partnership to market the software to airlines.

It took one month to write the basic program, with frequent modifications and upgrades made along the way. The business continues to thrive today with new products.

THE SECRET TO SUCCESS

Bair credits a couple things with his and his partner's success in the industry. First of all, they knew the industry. They had worked with the airline industry, understood how it operated, and were able to identify the gaps in its systems. This knowledge allowed him and his friend to develop products that were a perfect fit for the industry.

In addition, Bair already knew many of his customers, and they knew him. Building and maintaining good relationships is a vital part of any business. Bair's inside connections made it easier to get started and make his business grow.

DIG IN!

If you have hopes of becoming a computer programmer or of creating your own software programs, Bair suggests that you get started now. Get your own computer and aggressively teach yourself how to use it. Use it enough, and you'll figure out how it works.

He suggests that you write your own program in a simple programming environment such as Visual Basic. Use the training manuals and follow the examples they provide. Once you get the knack for it, you can make changes and add your ideas to customize your own miniprograms.

YOU EITHER HAVE IT OR YOU DON'T

Bair says that you'll see pretty quickly if this type of computer work is something you enjoy. The most important skill is an ability to think clearly and logically. This skill comes naturally to the most effective programmers. Even so, it's a skill that takes practice to perfect.

Systems Analyst

SHORTCUTS

GO find a company or government department that has a large computer system. Ask your computer teacher or parent to help you arrange a visit to see how its mainframe works.

READ *How Computers Work* by Ron White (Indianapolis, Ind.: Ziff Davis, 1997).

TRY choosing a computer system for your school. Read a few computer magazines, then imagine you have to recommend a system for your school.

SKILL SET

✔ COMPUTERS

✔ MATH

✔ SCIENCE

WHAT IS A SYSTEMS ANALYST?

A personal computer usually sits on a desktop—or perhaps on the floor with the monitor on the desk. It's a relatively simple machine, designed for use by one person at a time. Now imagine a huge computer system, one made up of several big computers connected together, perhaps housed in a special room, and being used by hundreds of people, perhaps even thousands, at the same time. These systems are called mainframes.

Many large companies have such systems, and the person who's in charge of keeping it all going is the systems analyst. Actually a system like this may require a team of system analysts to keep it running. These people are responsible for a variety of tasks.

Sometimes their work begins even before a computer system arrives at the company's offices. It's their job, for instance, to design the system that the company needs. They have to figure out how the computer system will be used and pick exactly the right system for the job. This is not as easy as it may sound. Go back to the single PC. It's fairly simple to decide what to get in an individual computer—the amount of memory, the type of screen, whether you want a modem or sound card, and so on. When it comes to the giant corporate computer system, things get quite a bit trickier. It takes someone with an extremely wide range of knowledge in areas such as software, hardware, programming, and networking to make the right choices.

Once the computer system arrives, it's the systems analyst's job to get it running and make sure it stays running. That's no easy task, either. In the personal computing world, when you want to use a new program, you simply install it and start using it. Installing software on mainframes can be a huge task. In some cases, it can take weeks of programming to get the software properly configured.

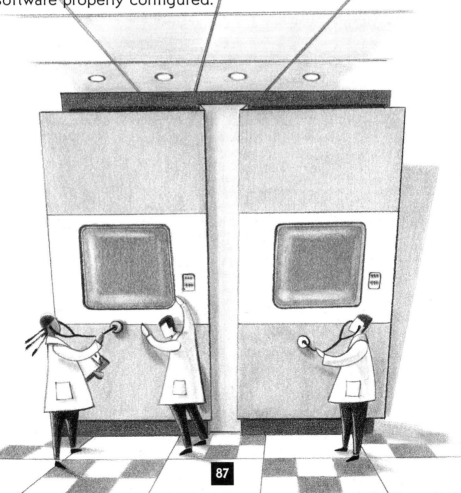

As of early 1998, however, about 80 percent of a systems analyst's work is likely to be fixing the year 2000 problem. Many old computers won't be able to handle dates in 2000, because they use two-digit years: They use 01 instead of 1901. So when the year changes from 99 to 00, the computers will read 1900, instead of 2000. This is a huge dilemma for the entire computer industry.

Another dilemma facing major corporations is that good systems analysts seem to be few and far between these days. Most newcomers to the computer business go into the PC side, partly because they are continuing a past misconception in the computer industry that huge systems would eventually disappear, leaving PCs to take over. It's now clear that that is not the case, that these large systems are here to stay. And, for the moment, that means there's plenty of work for systems administrators, and the pay is good.

To enter this line of work, certainly a college-level computer science program is very useful. The ability to program in languages such as Assembly, FORTRAN, COBOL, and PL/I helps as well, as they are languages used by these large systems. A systems analyst often starts as a personal-computer network systems administrator.

This is not the sort of job you go into directly from school. Rather, it takes plenty of experience; people tend to work their way into this job gradually. But, for computer experts who think that bigger is better, this is a field to consider!

TRY IT OUT

YOU'RE IN CONTROL

Spend a day in control of a computer system. You probably won't be able to get anywhere near a mainframe, but you may be able to help out in your school's computer lab. Perhaps you can help install new software, fix broken computers, and decide what needs to be done in order to upgrade the systems.

Many schools have a computer committee that meets in the evenings and does these things; ask if you can join in one evening. Otherwise talk with your computer teacher about helping out sometime.

YEAR 2000

By the time you get involved with mainframes and maybe even by the time you read this, the year 2000 problem (also known as Y2K) will be over, but it's a good example of the sort of major headaches that systems analysts have to deal with. You can find lots of information about this problem on the World Wide Web, at the following sites.

- Computer Date Crisis at http://www.everything2000. com/
- Sun—The Year 2000 Program at http://www.sun. com/y2000/
- Tick, Tick, Tick at http://www.tickticktick.com/
- Y2K Times at http://www.2k-times.com/
- The www.Y2K.com Web Site at http://www.y2k.com/

TEST A PROGRAM

A major task for systems analysts is the testing of software. They buy software, install it, modify it to fit their organization's needs, and then test it to make sure it works properly.

You can test software yourself by choosing a program—a game, word processor, or graphics program, for instance—then using it for a while. Write down any problems you find. If something just doesn't seem to work properly, write it down. Also write down things that just don't seem to make sense—menu-option names or command names that don't seem very understandable, procedures that seem more complicated than they need to be. Write a report explaining the problems and what should be done to fix the program.

CHECK IT OUT

Association of Information Technology Professionals (AITP)
315 South Northwest Highway, Suite 200
Park Ridge, Illinois 60068
Phone: 800-224-9371
E-mail: info@aitp.org
Web: http://www.aitp.org/

Institute for Certification of Computing Professionals (ICCP)
2200 East Devon Avenue, Suite 247
Des Plaines, Illinois 60018
Phone: 800-843-8227
E-mail: 74040.3722@compuserve.com
Web: http://www.iccp.org/

GET ACQUAINTED

Ron Kuhl, Systems Analyst

CAREER PATH

CHILDHOOD ASPIRATION: To be a policeman or firefighter.

FIRST JOB: An electronic warfare technician for the U.S. Navy.

CURRENT JOB: Systems programmer analyst for Lockheed Martin.

SEEING THE WORLD

Ron Kuhl spent a couple of years earning a business degree in college but finally decided he wasn't ready to settle down—he wanted to see the world first. So he joined the U.S. Navy and spent eight years enlisted, working as an electronic warfare technician. He traveled quite a bit, with postings to several places in the United States and overseas.

When Kuhl left the Navy he took a job with Westinghouse Electric, working in their gas turbine division. Gas turbines are machines used to generate electricity, and Kuhl worked in the research and development division, testing gas turbines and using computers to gather data.

Kuhl spent seven years at Westinghouse and learned a lot about computers while he was there; he went to night classes to learn programming and also took courses at work, including training on IBM mainframes. Next he worked for General Electric, which was eventually bought by a company named Martin Marietta; that company merged with Lockheed, so now he works for a company called Lockheed Martin and has been there about 12 years.

MAKING IT ALL FIT TOGETHER

At Lockheed, Kuhl works as a systems analyst, taking care of an IBM mainframe and its connections to the company's computer network. "We determine what kind of products we'll have to install on the system, what software packages, and so on. Then we have to make sure that the right software is purchased," he explains.

Most software that is installed on a mainframe must be customized in some way; it's not like installing an MS Windows program. These programs have to talk with other software packages. Making them all fit together can be major job— weeks of work sometimes.

THE YEAR 2000

At the time of this interview, a major responsibility of Kuhl's is the year 2000 problem. He is involved in updating software to make sure it will be able to handle four-digit dates properly. Kuhl has to determine how the problem will be handled, pick replacement software, install it, and then test and modify it.

He's also involved in integrating a new system, bringing data from another company that Lockheed Martin bought recently into their system. Each division of Lockheed Martin has a "partition" on the mainframe, a special area set aside for it. Lockheed Martin has tactical aircraft, missiles, and space divisions, for instance, and each one has its own computer resources.

A PROBLEM OR TWO

Kuhl enjoys his work, but there is a downside. "The time it takes to get anything done can be frustrating," he says. "And the documentation we have to work with is almost always pretty bad." As Kuhl knows, programmers explain to technical writers how their programs work. The problem is that the writers don't always understand the technical side of things. It often takes a lot of effort to determine from their documentation how the programs work.

There's the overtime too. Kuhl says that when they need to test new products or put something into operation, there's always a lot of overtime—and "of course it has to be on weekends." These sorts of procedures have to be carried out on weekends because that's when most people are at home—so the computer system isn't being used so much.

All in all, however, he enjoys this job—especially all the variety. He also appreciates having the chance to work with smart and interesting people.

Systems Manager

TAKE A TRIP!

Systems Manager

SHORTCUTS

SKILL SET

✔ BUSINESS
✔ TALKING
✔ COMPUTERS

GO talk with the person in charge of computers and technology for your school district.

READ the *Computer Dictionary for Beginners* by Anna Claybourne (Tulsa, Okla.: EDC Publishing, 1996).

TRY creating a chart listing the components that a top-notch computer system requires and then visiting stores in your area to find the very best deal.

WHAT IS A SYSTEMS MANAGER?

Running a major computer system is almost like running a military operation. There's a huge team of people involved, and the systems manager has to make sure that everything comes together in the right way at the right time. He or she is responsible for the overall management of the system. The systems manager may not actually work directly with computers, but is in charge of all the people who do. You could say that the systems manager is the computer boss.

Systems management is all about managing people and resources. You don't "get your hands dirty" in this job. Systems managers don't program or install computers; they tell other people how and when to do these things. Good people skills such as talking and listening are key to this job. Another big part is research—learning about new products in order to make the best decisions about building the most effective system. Business sense is a plus since the job can also involve some pretty hefty budgets.

And when something goes wrong with the system, the systems manager is the one most likely to be held responsible, which is why this type of work generally requires quite a bit

93

of previous experience. Systems managers typically start off as programmers or systems analysts.

If this is the sort of job you might aspire to, start by gaining the technical knowledge you need. A computer science degree, coupled with experience in programming or computer networking, can be a great start. You'll eventually have to get some business training and experience as well. Many people take business courses in the evenings, working to earn an MBA (a master's degree in business administration) while working full-time.

TRY IT OUT

BACKGROUND KNOWLEDGE

Projects costing tens or hundreds of millions of dollars are bound to entail the use of many different technologies, so background knowledge is very important for a systems manager. There are many books available that will give you a good overall view of the computer business. Try some of the following:

———————————

Derfler, Frank J., and Les Freed. *How Networks Work.* Indianapolis, Ind.: Ziff Davis, 1996

Gralla, Preston. *How the Internet Works.* Indianapolis, Ind.: Ziff Davis, 1996

Gralla, Preston, and Mina Reimer. *How Intranets Work.* Indianapolis, Ind.: Ziff Davis, 1996

White, Ron. *How Computers Work.* Indianapolis, Ind.: Ziff Davis, 1997

———————————

EVALUATE A TECHNOLOGY

Pick a new technology and evaluate the benefits to your school. Let's say you pick speech-recognition software. Begin by creating a list of ways in which such software might help at school: Students unable to type could write memos by speaking, the computers can be controlled by voice, and so on. Read as many articles as you can find on the subject.

Check the major computer magazines at your local library to see if any have done product reviews related to the technology you are evaluating, and write down any new benefits and problems you can find. For example, voice technology doesn't actually work well: It's very slow, it makes many mistakes, and so on. Finally, write a small summary. Is this technology really likely to help or will it be a waste of money?

GET A HEAD START

Because you can't go straight into systems management, you need to start somewhere else, so make sure you read the following chapters in this book.

Computer Programmer
Internet Systems Administrator
Software Entrepreneur
Systems Analyst

CHECK IT OUT

Association for Computing Machinery (ACM)
1515 Broadway, 17th Floor
New York, New York 10036-5701
E-mail: acmhelp@acm.org
Web: http://www.acm.org/

Association for Systems Management World Wide (ASMWW)
3B25 Kimlane Road
Gibsonia, Pennsylvania 15046-9781
E-mail: rkellywiz@aol.com
Web: http://www.infoanalytic.com/asm/in/index.htm

GET ACQUAINTED

Timothy Vann, Systems Manager

CAREER PATH

CHILDHOOD ASPIRATION: To work with electronic equipment.

FIRST JOB: Cleaning wire out of farm equipment in the Kansas heat.

CURRENT JOB: Field operations manager at AT&T Wireless Service.

A LITTLE DETOUR ALONG THE WAY

Having been raised on a farm, Timothy Vann was always fascinated with equipment of all kinds, particularly electronic devices. He was the one his siblings would look for when something needed to be fixed. He came to his current career after trying out several ventures.

Vann left home after high school and attended a junior college. His education was cut short by a serious car accident that required a steel plate being placed in his leg (he still has problems getting through security at airports) and a long recovery period. Upon his recuperation (and marriage to a young woman back home), he began in earnest the pursuit of his career.

From his hometown to Phoenix, Phoenix to Kansas City, Kansas City to Denver, Denver to Oklahoma City, and back to Denver, Vann was in pursuit of his dream job. Along the way, he attended technical schools and built storage sheds to pay for his education. After scrimping and saving, he finished an accelerated course at a technical institute and graduated with an associate degree in 18 months.

THE PURSUIT CONTINUES

The cellular phone industry was in its infancy when, through a stroke of luck and the help of a mentor, Vann obtained a job with a new cellular phone company as a "drive test person." Many miles were put on his vehicle as he drove around the state, collecting data to plot coverage maps and dealing with interference issues. He then was promoted to an information systems technician, installing phone systems and data system work stations.

MORE EXCITEMENT TO COME

Through hard work, long hours, and perseverance, Vann was promoted to systems technician, working on equipment in the field. From this he advanced to senior systems technician and is now the field operations manager. He has a cellular phone with him at all times as he supervises and manages people who do the day-to-day repair and maintenance on the hundreds of cellular sites across his statewide territory in Colorado.

SQUIRREL CATASTROPHES

Every day brings new challenges. There are no "typical" days for Vann. There are always glitches of one kind or another—software glitches that cause hardware failures, for instance. And, an occasional squirrel chewing on coaxial cables can knock out service in an entire city!

Technical Support Representative

SHORTCUTS

SKILL SET

✔ COMPUTERS

✔ TALKING

✔ WRITING

GO call a software program's technical support number with a question about the program.

READ *The Complete Idiot's Guide to PCs* by Joe Kraynak (Indianapolis: Que, 1997) or *Mac OS 8 for Dummies* by Bob Levitus (Indianapolis: IDG, 1997). Both provide a great way to get to know your computer.

TRY volunteering to help the teacher in charge of the school's computer lab—there's always something to fix or install.

WHAT IS A TECHNICAL SUPPORT REPRESENTATIVE?

Technical support representatives—also known as help desk techs—are computer experts who answer questions about computer programs or computer hardware. If you've spent much time working with computers, you may have already discovered that it is a good idea to have help available around the clock. (For some strange reason, computers never seem to crash during business hours!)

There are two types of businesses in which teams of technical support representatives work. One place is at companies that produce or publish specific types of computer software or hardware. For instance, if a program you are working in starts doing weird things, you can call the company that produces it and ask them what to do to fix it. Or, if you are trying to install a new modem in your computer, you could call the company that makes the modem and ask how to make it work. While the techs that work in places like these must have a good overall understanding of computers, they must be whizzes at working with the specific product they represent.

Another place you are likely to find technical support representatives is at any good-size company that uses computers. The people working at these companies depend on their in-house techs to bail them out of all sorts of computer problems, so you can imagine that they have to know their way around quite an assortment of equipment and applications.

Of course, having someone sitting by the phone waiting for customers to call is a very expensive way to fix problems, so most companies regard it as a last resort—or even charge customers who consult the technical support department. Instead, many companies now take care of the most common problems with recorded messages detailing how to fix them. Many companies also have documents that can be faxed to their customers.

But the telephone is not the only tool used to help customers fix their problems. These days many companies are also using e-mail, websites, and Internet or on-line service discussion groups as ways to get information to their customers.

How does all this innovation affect technical support representatives? Not so long ago, the tech simply provided help over the telephone line. That's still an important part of the job, but now so is answering e-mail, writing documents to be placed at a website or to be added to the fax-on-demand system, and answering questions in Internet discussion groups or chat rooms. Small companies in particular also use technical support staff to test new products, since they are so in tune with how consumers might use them.

You don't need a degree to get into this business. Employers are looking for people who enjoy working with computers and who have a wide range of knowledge about different software and hardware systems; in short, they want people who are comfortable around computers. Communication skills are important, too. It's one thing to be a computer expert and quite another to be able to communicate your knowledge in a way that a typical computer user can understand. Strong verbal and written skills are a must for this type of work.

The job involves equal parts of working with computers and helping people. It helps if you enjoy both and are eager to keep learning new things. Technology changes rapidly, and you'll have to stay a step ahead of it to offer the best support to your customers.

TRY IT OUT

TECH FOR HIRE

Isn't it a great feeling to be able to do something that the adults around you can't do? It seems that your generation has the edge on all this technology. Many adults are computer illiterate, barely able to turn on the computer much less do something useful with it.

That's where you come in. Find one of these adults and volunteer to teach him or her the basics. Your potential "customers" might include a parent or grandparent, a neighbor or even a teacher.

You might explain how to open program and files in Microsoft Windows or how to work with a word processor. You'll find that things you think are obvious are not clear to someone who has no experience with computers, so think carefully about how you explain things. Be as clear as possible, and avoid using computer jargon whenever possible.

COMPUTER TUTOR

Chances are pretty good that your school has a computer lab. Ask your computer teacher if they'd like some help working with students who are having trouble catching on. You might find time to do so during the school day or set up regular hours before or after school. You'll learn a lot about computers and get some great experience to add to your résumé.

CYBER SUBSCRIBE

Read a computer magazine or two each month to stay current on what's happening. You should find a few on hand at the local library. Find one or two that do a good job explaining things in simple terms and save up your money to buy your own subscription. Some magazines to try include

Family PC
P.O. Box 55411
Boulder, Colorado 80323-5411
http://www.familypc.com/

Home PC
P.O. Box 420211
Palm Coast, Florida 32142-0211
http://www.homepc.com/

Mac Home v
P.O. Box 469
Mt. Morris, Illinois 61054-7971
http://www.machome.com/

PC Novice/Smart Computer
P.O. Box 85380
Lincoln, Nebraska 68501-9807
http://www.smartcomputing.com/

FIND A PERSONAL COMPUTER USERS GROUP

Most medium- and large-size cities have personal computer user groups. These are generally run by one or two knowledgeable people, but most members are just trying to learn. Through these groups you can get to play with new software programs at no cost—they often have software libraries—and to learn about a wide range of computer-related subjects. Track one down through your local computer paper, ask at a computer store, or contact the Association of Personal Computer User Groups (see under Check It Out). Most will be happy to have younger members.

CHECK IT OUT

Association of Personal Computer User Groups (APCUG)
4020 McEwen, Suite 105
Dallas, Texas 75244-5019
Phone: 972-233-9107, ext. 207
E-mail: office@apcug.org
Web: http://www.apcug.org/

Association of Support Professionals (ASP)
17 Main Street
Watertown, Massachusetts 02172-4491
Phone: 617-924-3944, ext. 14
Fax: 617-924-7288
E-mail: pdwen@softletter.com
Web: http://www.asponline.com/

Software Support Professionals Association (SSPA)
1755 Telstar Drive, Suite 101
Colorado Springs, Colorado 80920-1017
Phone: 800-653-9653
E-mail: sspa@sbforums.com
Web: http://www.sspa-online.com/

GET ACQUAINTED

Elias AbuGhazaleh, Technical
Support Representative

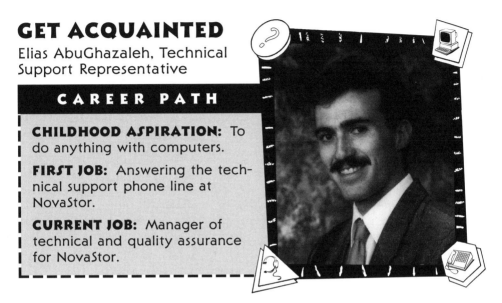

CAREER PATH

CHILDHOOD ASPIRATION: To
do anything with computers.

FIRST JOB: Answering the technical support phone line at
NovaStor.

CURRENT JOB: Manager of
technical and quality assurance
for NovaStor.

LOVE AT FIRST BYTE

Elias AbuGhazaleh decided that he wanted to work with computers when he was 12, when he first used an Apple personal
computer. He wasn't really quite sure what he wanted to do,
but he knew it had to be something involving computers. "I
used to hack programs in the evenings after school and
learned a lot of different programs and systems," he says. By
the time he reached high school, he realized—or, at least,
thought he realized—that he wanted to be a computer programmer.

Things didn't quite turn out the way he expected, though.
He went to the California Lutheran University to earn a computer science degree, intending to become a programmer
when he graduated. During his senior year he took a part-
time job with NovaStor Corporation, answering their technical support calls. NovaStor sells backup, encryption, and
anti-virus software, and it was AbuGhazaleh's job to help
NovaStor's clients figure out how to fix any problems they
might have with these programs.

WHAT NEXT?

After graduating, AbuGhazaleh took a full-time position with NovaStor working in technical support but hoping to move into a programming position when one became available. But that programming position never did become available. Instead, NovaStor promoted him to manager of the technical support department and added another responsibility too: to manage the company's quality assurance department. That's the department that tests the company's products and ensures that they are working correctly. AbuGhazaleh believes that these two functions—technical support and quality assurance—should always be linked, although in large companies they're generally two very separate departments. Ideally, however, people who sit and talk with customers all day, learning about problems with the products, should also be involved with testing products and recommending changes to those products. After all, these people know what customers want and what customers find frustrating about the company's products. AbuGhazaleh rotates staff between the two departments, letting his seven technical support people help test and recommend changes to products and making his quality assurance people spend time talking to customers on the technical support line.

NO REGRETS

AbuGhazaleh never did become a programmer, but he has no regrets. "I'm a people person," he says. "I like the interaction with customers, helping them fix their problems." If he'd become a programmer he may have found himself more isolated, spending hours alone in front of his computer terminal. In fact seeing programmers at work has convinced him that programming may have been the wrong choice for him, and that luck led him to the right career.

"This is a great company to work for," says AbuGhazaleh. "It's a small company—around 40 people—and I'm glad now that I didn't go to work for a large company." What does AbuGhazaleh see down the road? He'd like to get more involved in engineering and the development of new products, natural extensions of what he's doing now. He finds that being closely involved with the problems a product may have helps him see where products may be improved.

THE REAL PICTURE

No job is perfect, and even this one has its frustrations. "There's never enough time in the day," says AbuGhazaleh, "and sometimes it's difficult dealing with problems that you know can't be fixed and explaining to the customer that there is no solution." But AbuGhazaleh is happy to be where he is now. The computer industry is an exciting one. It's the future: "Computers are everywhere. Everything involves computers these days; I can't imagine why anyone wouldn't want to be involved in this business."

AbuGhazaleh has a degree in computer science, but he recognizes that kids can get into the technical support business without one. "Fool around with computers," he says. "You need to be up to date with the computer industry, have a wide range of knowledge, understand all the jargon, and be capable of talking with people intelligently."

Technical Writer

SHORTCUTS

SKILL SET

✔ COMPUTERS

✔ WRITING

✔ SCIENCE

GO visit the Society for Technical Communication's website (http://stc.org/).

READ *The Elements of Style* by William Strunk and E. B. White. It will help you learn to write clearly and concisely.

TRY writing some instructions for a product you use, perhaps a product that came with terrible documentation.

WHAT IS A TECHNICAL WRITER?

Have you ever tried to use a computer program's user manual and thought you could describe how to use the program better? Well, maybe you should consider a career in technical writing. A technical writer can do any number of things: write user manuals for computer programs, instructions for using complicated telecommunications equipment, and information that will be published on a website. Technical writers write about all sorts of products and processes, which is one of the nice things about this career: There's a lot of variety.

Technical writers explain how to use things or do things, and as the items we use every day seem to be getting more complicated, there's a lot of explaining to do. For every computer, computer program, telephone, answering machine, printer, scanner, fax machine, car, motorbike, watch, calculator, or whatever else you can imagine, instructions have to be written. Instructions are also required for many toys, bicycles, and games. The instructions produced by technical writers may fit on a single piece of paper, or they may take up thousands of pages in a several volumes of loose-leaf binders.

Technical writing is the sort of job that tends to expand too. Your employer may need someone to write some promotional materials—brochures or flyers, for instance. If the company doesn't have a public relations or advertising writer (and most don't), you may be asked to step in and create these things. Writers often work on websites too; in fact, many webmasters start off as technical writers.

Technical writers often write proposals, special documents used by companies when looking to start a new venture. A proposal describes what the company will do for a client, often in great detail. Technical writers sometimes write magazine articles designed to promote their companies, and some write the computer books you see for sale in your local bookstore.

A good technical writer must be able to write well. But just as important is the ability to structure the flow of information. You may be able to write the most beautiful prose, but unless you can explain things in a clear and logical manner, you won't be a good technical writer. You must be able to learn quickly too. If you're

the sort of person who finds it difficult to pick up new ideas and learn how to use new products, this probably isn't the career for you. But if you really enjoy the challenge of learning new things, you'll feel at home with technical writing.

This is a booming business, with the demand for technical writers growing rapidly. Consequently it's fairly well paid, and there are lots of opportunities for freelancers. If at some point in your career you decide you want to work for yourself, you may be able to build a successful freelance technical writing business, as many others have done.

Most technical writers do not have technical writing degrees; such degrees are relatively new, and most of the more senior writers just fell into technical writing, almost by accident. Many journalists become technical writers (because it's much better paid), as do geologists, biologists, programmers, people with business or English degrees—just about anyone. Still, if you're interested in this career, you should think about getting a technical writing degree. A computer science degree would also be useful and would provide you with more flexibility in your career choice later. There are also a number of correspondence courses on technical writing, which could be combined with a course in computer science.

TRY IT OUT

USE THE INTERNET

There is a lot of information about technical writing on the World Wide Web and in Internet mailing-list discussion groups. Try the website for Peter Kent's book *Making Money in Technical Writing;* the address is http://www.mcp. com/mgr/arco/techwr/. There you'll find a page containing hundreds of links to useful websites, grouped by the chapter in which the links are mentioned in the book. In Chapter 24, under the Working Online heading, you'll find information about the technical writer's discussion groups. Subscribe to one or two (in particular the group named techwr-l) and see what people have to say. (Instructions are included on how to subscribe to each group.) And don't be shy—ask a question or two!

CONTACT THE STC

The Society for Technical Communication (STC) is the world's largest organization for technical writers, with more than 15,000 members. There are local chapters in most large North American cities; contact the headquarters, or see their website to find a chapter near you (see under Check It Out). Call someone and chat for a few minutes. They'll be happy to talk with you, and although you'll find that all the members are adults, you might want to sit in on a meeting or two.

READ THESE BOOKS

See if your library has or can get a copy of *Clear Technical Writing* by John A. Brogan (New York: McGraw-Hill, 1973) and *The Complete Guide to Writing Software User Manuals* by Brad M. McGehee (Cincinnati: Writer's Digest Books, 1984). The first provides a great way to clean up your writing and make it sharp and clear, while the second is a wonderful primer on writing computer user guides. (The library is the best place to find these books, as the first is very expensive, and the second is out of print.) For a look at the freelance technical writing business, read *Making Money in Technical Writing* by Peter Kent (New York: ARCO, 1997). You could also visit a large bookstore, which should have several books about technical writing.

TRY FOR YOURSELF

The best way to discover whether or not you would enjoy technical writing is to do a little. Technical writing is all about writing instructions—about anything. Get some practice: Volunteer to write announcements about meetings and events held by a school club. Make sure you provide all the information people will need, and make sure all the information is easy to read and to understand. Don't use too many words; see how cutting unnecessary words from your writing makes it clearer. Use short words that everyone can understand and that are not likely to confuse. And play a little with different line spacing, font sizes, and font styles, to create a document that provides the information as clearly as possible.

CHECK IT OUT

Institute of Electrical and Electronic Engineers/Professional
  Communication Society (IEEE-PCS)
IEEE Service Center
P.O. Box 1331
Piscataway, New Jersey 08854
Web: http://www.ieee.org/society/pcs/

Society for Documentation Professionals
214 Liberty Square
Danvers, Massachusetts 01923
E-mail: RJLIPPINCOTT@delphi.com
Web: http://www.sdpro.org/

Society for Technical Communication
901 North Stuart Street
Arlington, Virginia 22203
E-mail: stc@tmn.com
Web: http://stc.org/

Special Interest Group for DOCumentation (SIGDOC) of the
  Association for Computing Machinery
c/o ACM
P.O. Box 12115
Church Street Station
New York, New York 10249
E-mail: acmhelp@acm.org
Web: http://www.acm.org/sigdoc/

GET ACQUAINTED

Brenda Dickson Curry,
Technical Writer

CAREER PATH

CHILDHOOD ASPIRATION: To be a veterinarian.

FIRST JOB: Scheduling ads at a radio station.

CURRENT JOB: Freelance technical writer.

A CHANGE OF PLANS

Brenda Curry has always enjoyed writing. In elementary school she used to write poems and read them in class. But originally she wanted to be a vet because she loved animals so.

By college, she was studying business but soon found that she preferred her elective journalism courses (and got better grades in them—a great clue for knowing you're on the right track). In her sophomore year at the University of Houston, she changed her major. She graduated with a major in journalism and a minor in English, specializing in public relations and advertising.

Before graduating, however, Curry had already uncovered her talent. The Harris County Child Protective Services department asked the students in her college advertising class to write ads encouraging people to adopt minority children. Each student wrote a piece, and everyone voted for the best one. Curry's ad won and was produced for television.

RADIO WRITING

Encouraged by the success of her first television piece, Curry decided to go into copywriting—the business of writing ads. But, she found it to be a hard business to break into, with jobs few and far between. "The mistake I made was not taking an internship while in college," she says. "It's a good way to graduate with some experience in the job you want."

So, instead of going into copywriting, Curry began work at a radio station. She'd hoped for the chance to investigate and report about consumer complaints but got stuck in scheduling ads instead. Frustrated with waiting for the consumer reports program, she moved on and took an editing job working for a NASA subcontractor.

This company, Computer Sciences Corporation, was creating software and related documentation for NASA mission control and the Apollo program. Curry began by editing a variety of technical books. The first was on something called a thermal vacuuming system.

WRITING AT LAST

Curry was soon promoted from editing to writing. She got a raise and her first technical writing job. She worked for NASA for about three years, and then she took a job with the Texas Agricultural Extension Service, writing a newsletter and producing workshops. That lasted about six years. Next she returned to NASA for seven years, and finally, moved from Houston to Dallas to be with her family.

Her first job in Dallas was working through a technical service agency at Spring, the telecommunications giant. Technical service agencies find temporary staff for companies and hire many technical writers. Contracts often last for years, although they can sometimes be canceled at very short notice. In fact, when the Spring contract was canceled after three months, Curry was devastated. She'd never imagined she was leaving a long-term position with NASA for something that would last just a few weeks!

FREELANCE—A GREAT WAY TO GO

Things bounced back quickly enough, though, and Curry is glad that she decided to stick with freelance writing. She's worked almost exclusively on contract for the last ten years, working for companies such as Data General, Texas Instruments, Ericsson, Mobil, and Nortel. The work is plentiful, and it pays better than full-time technical writing positions.

As a mother, she likes the flexible hours too. She's able to attend school meetings and schedule doctor's appointments during the day and easily make up the time later.

She finds the job interesting and enjoys making the research, the writing, the page layout, and editing come together like a giant puzzle. Curry finds satisfaction in getting them all together just right.

Trainer

SHORTCUTS

SKILL SET

✔ TALKING

✔ COMPUTERS

✔ WRITING

GO take every opportunity you can to talk in front of your class.

READ *I Can See You Naked* by Ron Hoff (Kansas City: Andrews & McMeel, 1995).

TRY learning a new program or computer game and teaching your friends, step-by-step, how to work with the program.

WHAT IS A TRAINER?

In this world of rapidly changing computer technology, an education doesn't end when you leave high school or even college. Millions of people have had to learn completely new skills, long after they thought their education was over.

On the technology side of things, the computer trainer is responsible for teaching people new skills. Trainers are sometimes employed by large corporations. A company with thousands of employees always has someone who needs training, so such companies can afford to have a full-time training department. Smaller companies, however, use the services of computer training companies, another major employer of trainers. These companies often have their own office buildings, with several classrooms full of computers. Sometimes they do on-site training too; that is, they send trainers to a company's building and train the employees there. Some companies also market their courses directly to individuals, renting large rooms in various cities to carry out one- or two-day seminars. And many trainers start their own businesses. As with a number of careers in computing, training is an ideal freelance occupation.

A good trainer is a people person, someone who enjoys working with people all day. Many trainers have a great deal of technical experience, but they've discovered they prefer working with people rather than with machines. Other trainers knew right from the start what they wanted to do, and they have learned the technical knowledge they need so that they can train others.

If you're interested in a training career, you'll have to be comfortable talking in front of groups of people; that's what you'll be doing for most of your time, after all. A strong computing background is important too, but there's generally no requirement to have a computer science degree in order to get started in this career. Many trainers have no degree of any kind. Teaching abilities are more important than technical knowledge: Often training companies will teach you what you need to know, as long as they believe you have the skills and personality to be a good trainer. And because there's such a wide range of information that has to be taught, there's room for trainers of varying backgrounds and technical abilities. Advanced programming courses, for example, must be taught by someone with a strong programming

COMPUTING
101

background. But courses on how to use a word processor or spreadsheet can be taught by any capable trainer, once he or she has learned the program.

You need to be outgoing, understanding, and *patient.* Teaching can be a difficult job, and sometimes you need the patience to allow students to absorb things (ask your teachers about this!). You also must be able to break down complicated subjects into smaller, easier-to-understand blocks. A good trainer can quickly see how a subject is made up of smaller parts, then teaches those parts one by one.

Learn as much about computers as you can, and perhaps focus on one area you enjoy: graphics software, desktop-publishing software, or website authoring software, for instance. The more you know about computers in general, however, the more attractive you will be to employers. Having been employed in a retail computer store helps, as such work provides a good overall view of personal computing, both hardware and software, and gives you lots of contact with the public.

TRY IT OUT

VISIT TRAINING COMPANIES ON-LINE

Visit a few training companies on-line, and see what sort of services and classes they provide. They're not hard to find; literally hundreds, probably thousands, have set up websites. Here's how to find them: Go to Yahoo! (http://www.yahoo.com/), and search for *computer training.* Then click on the following links: Business and Economy; Companies; Computers; Services; Training.

You'll see a page with hundreds of links to training companies around the world. Visit some of these sites, and look at the types of subjects they are running training courses on. Read the course descriptions too so that you get an idea of the information covered in each course, and the depth to which each lesson goes. You may even find that you know enough to teach some of these courses! Many introductory courses teach *very* basic stuff to adults who feel that they are getting left behind by the computer revolution.

Follow the Job Opportunities or Trainers Needed links that you'll see on some sites, too. These will take you to pages with information about the trainers they need and the skills those trainers must have.

SIGN UP FOR CLASSES

Why not take a class yourself? Many community colleges have low-cost computing courses. Simply pick a course that interests you and attend. You'll learn something about the subject being taught, of course, but you'll also get to see a trainer in action.

Make sure you chat with the trainer a little, and explain that you're interested in computer training. Write a report card on the trainer (just for you, of course, don't give it to the trainer!). Note what you liked about the way the trainer taught the course and what you didn't like. Was he or she too quick, rushing through subjects, or did the trainer take the time to explain each concept before moving on to the next? Did the trainer seem to have a good understanding of the subject and be able to explain it in an accessible way? Or did the trainer sound like he or she was teaching a subject without fully understanding it? Think about how the lesson went, and write down what you would have done to make it work better.

TEACH YOUNGER KIDS

Ask your computer teacher if you can help teach some of the younger kids in your school. This will be great experience in patience! Teaching young kids can be very challenging because they often have short attention spans. Your task is to try as hard as you can to teach them how to use a program, such as a math game, a word processor, or graphics program, while accepting the fact that they may not be listening quite as closely as you'd like.

And remember, break concepts down into little steps, then teach the steps one by one.

CHECK IT OUT

ITTA (Information Technology Training Association)
8400 North MoPac Expressway, Suite 201
Austin, Texas 78759
E-mail: plaird@itta.org
Web: http://www.itta.org/

GET ACQUAINTED

Molly Roberts, Trainer

CAREER PATH

CHILDHOOD ASPIRATION: To be president of the United States or a doctor.

FIRST JOB: Graphic designer.

CURRENT JOB: Internet instructor for Prosoft.

TAKING CARE OF BUSINESS

Molly Roberts has always kept busy; she had her first part-time job when she was 11 working as a junior counselor at a day camp. She worked as the office manager in her mother's real estate business, too, which is where she first used computers. She used the computer to calculate loans and enter real estate listings, and she ended up spending plenty of time with the user manuals and on-line help.

Roberts studied English and political science in college and was thinking of going on to law school. But when she heard that most law students never become lawyers anyway—many go into research or become lobbyists—she changed her mind. Instead she took a job with a bank, as a graphic designer in their investment division. She had to use investment statistics to create charts and graphs for presentations; the job required strong computing experience, and Roberts was interested in investing, so it seemed a good fit.

A JOB WITH THE BANK

Roberts stayed with the bank for about 18 months and then worked for herself for about 8 months doing internet design—creating World Wide Web pages. But she found marketing herself and running the business at the same time difficult, so when she saw an ad from Prosoft looking for trainers, she jumped at the opportunity. Prosoft needed people-oriented people; the company could teach the technical skills, they said, but the most important thing was for the trainers to be comfortable working with people.

Roberts had a feeling that this was the perfect job for her. She's since discovered that she was right, and she's never been happier with a job than she is now. She travels a lot, all over the United States, from California to New York to Texas. She teaches people about HTML (HyperText Markup Language, the "coding" system used to create World Wide Web pages), multimedia, website creation software, and even about JavaScript (a scripting language used on many websites).

IT'S SHOWBIZ

Roberts feels that she's part entertainer. "If you don't like to talk in front of people, avoid this career," she says. "You have to be able to get up in front of room full of people and entertain them; training is part teaching and part showbiz." A good trainer doesn't just recite a list of facts. You have to make the training session—the "show"—interesting and lively.

"This can be a challenging job," Roberts says. "You often have people from a wide variety of backgrounds and computer experience in the same class, so you have to keep the experts happy while not losing the novices." This is especially true of the Internet, her specialty. Because it's so new, it's difficult to get a class full of people at the same technical level. "You need to be flexible, able to change the flow of the class at any moment. Whenever I start a lesson, I have seven different game plans I can follow, just in case."

Roberts expects to continue in training for now, though she'd like to branch out a little. She'd like to write courseware, the lesson plans that trainers work from, and might also enjoy writing training manuals, books used by individuals to train themselves. For the moment, however, she feels that she's in the right job at the right time.

Webmaster

SHORTCUTS

SKILL SET

✔ ART

✔ COMPUTERS

✔ WRITING

GO keep track of a favorite site on a regular basis to see how the webmaster keeps things fresh and exciting.

READ Internet websites—visit all different kinds!

TRY setting up a home page for your school.

WHAT IS A WEBMASTER?

A webmaster is . . . well, it depends on whom you ask. Some people put together a basic one-page home page on the Internet and declare themselves webmasters. In fact, if you look at all the homemade pages credited to "webmasters," you might get the idea that this is the fastest growing profession on the planet. It's a growing profession all right, but it's not quite as easy as it might look on the surface.

A webmaster is someone who creates websites on the World Wide Web. Webmasters apply a number of skills and resources to design, create, and maintain effective websites on behalf of their own companies, an employer, or any number of clients. The skills required vary widely. At a minimum, the webmaster must be able to create websites, so graphic design and writing skills are useful here. Webmasters may also be involved in promoting the website—that is, "getting the word out" so that people visit the site—requiring skills such as marketing and project management.

A few webmasters take over the role of web-server administrator, as well; that is, they not only create the website, but even keep the web server running. For that, the ability to set up and maintain network connections is needed. It's no wonder that many of the larger and more complex websites are actually run by a team of professionals.

For the most part, webmasters wear three hats: information manager, HTML-page creator (a page creator in HyperText Markup Language), and graphic designer. As information manager, the webmaster is responsible for the thoughtful arrangement of large volumes of information. Think of this part of the process as if the webmaster were an information architect, having to arrange all the information in "rooms" and create a blueprint so that visitors can easily find their way to the information they need.

As HTML-page creator, the webmaster places the information into a form that can be displayed by a web browser. HyperText Markup Language is the text-formatting language that all websites are written in. HTML uses simple codes to describe how each piece of text in a page should be displayed in a browser. It's relatively easy to learn—it's not like learning a programming language, which can be quite difficult—but there's quite a lot to it.

There are many programs that automatically create the pages. These are like word-processing programs for websites; you type the words, and the program enters the HTML codes for you. Nonetheless, most webmasters themselves understand quite a bit of HTML, as the HTML programs are often limited to a relatively small set of HTML commands. To get really creative, a webmaster must understand how to go beyond the programs and must enter some of the more advanced codes directly.

As graphic designer, the webmaster uses icons, graphics, color, and other elements of design to create an appealing look for the website. With millions of websites to choose from, competition keeps this phase of the process vital. The designer must create a unique identity that reflects the purpose of the site and the image that the client wishes to convey. With an ever-increasing amount of business being conducted on the Internet, the website is often the only contact a potential client has with a company, so it is especially important to make a good impression. Keeping the site fresh and exciting while maintaining a consistent look and feel are ongoing challenges for the webmaster.

Even though the career didn't even exist 10 years ago, opportunities for talented webmasters look promising for the future. There are no specific educational requirements for a webmaster, but the need for strong computer skills is obvious. Perhaps not so obvious is the need for equally strong communication skills. A degree in computer science can be a useful asset for a webmaster, but there's also room for the self-motivated, self-taught mavericks who continue to make an indelible mark on the computer profession.

TRY IT OUT

TALK THE TALK

HTML is the universal language of webmasters. For a free introduction to HTML, you can download the "Beginner's Guide to HTML" from the Internet. This useful resource is published by The National Center for Supercomputing Applications and can be found at this address: http://www. ncsa.uiuc.edu/General/Internet/WWW/HTMLPrimer.html.

Another helpful site for beginners was set up by the Johnson family and provides links to all kinds of resources for developing websites, including HTML tutorials and tips and graphics that can be downloaded into your own pages. You can visit the Johnsons' site here: http://www.dallas.net/kjohn64/computer.html.

MAKE A PLAN

Put on the webmaster's information manager hat, and gather all the information you can about your school. You might include the school directory, yearbook, newsletters, staff résumés, sports schedules, and calendar of special events. Use poster board to make a blueprint of what information you'd include and how you'd organize it so that visitors could find the good stuff quickly and easily.

START A VIRTUAL LIBRARY

There are several on-line resources that will keep you up to date with the latest technology and trends affecting the Web. Whenever possible, print out copies of helpful information and articles and keep them in a binder or folder.

Start creating your reference book with a stop at one of the Web's best sites for webmasters, the Webmaster's Notebook (http://www.cio.com/WebMaster/wm_notebook.html). Here you'll find the latest in categories such as essentials, graphics, HTML information, plug-ins, programming, and search engines.

There's also the Web Developer's Virtual Library (http://www.stars.com/), a gold mine of media kits, tutorials, and examples of especially well-designed sites. And take a look at your local library too; it's bound to have lots of books on HTML and website development.

LEARN THE ROPES

One of the best ways to learn anything is to watch those who do it in action. Watching the best webmasters do their thing is made easier by various web awards sites, such as these:

⚘ The Webmaster Awards at http://www.marketme.com/awards/

☼ The Best of the Web at http://www.botw.org/
☼ Beatrice's Web Guide at http://www.bguide.com/

Before you visit the week's award-winning sites, use blank sheets of paper to make simple charts for recording your reaction to the site. Include space to list answers to the following questions.

What do you like best about the site?
What don't you like about the site?
Why do you think they won the award?

Be sure that you give the site your own rating, and think about the techniques the webmaster used to create a good site. You might take a look at some really *bad* websites, too, which you can find through "worst of the web" award sites such as these:

☼ The Useless Pages at http://www.go2net.com/internet/
useless/
☼ Anthony's Most Annoying of the Web at http://www.
annoyances.com/annoying.html

CHECK IT OUT

HTML Writer's Guild
Web: http://www.hwg.org/

International Interactive Communications Society
10160 Southwest Nimbus Avenue, Suite F2
Portland, Oregon 97223
Web: http://www.iics.org/

National Webmasters Association
9580 Oak Avenue Parkway, Suite 7-177
Folsom, California 95630
Web: http://www.naw.org/

Webmasters Guild
P.O. Box 381231
Cambridge, Massachusetts 02238
Web: http://www.webmaster.org/

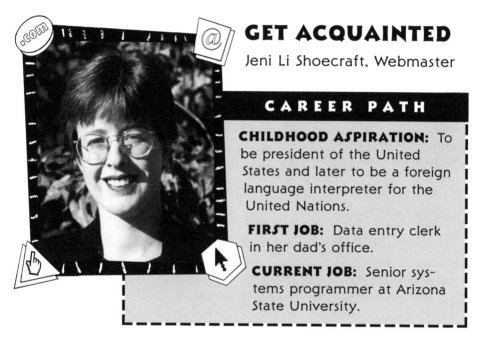

GET ACQUAINTED

Jeni Li Shoecraft, Webmaster

CAREER PATH

CHILDHOOD ASPIRATION: To be president of the United States and later to be a foreign language interpreter for the United Nations.

FIRST JOB: Data entry clerk in her dad's office.

CURRENT JOB: Senior systems programmer at Arizona State University.

WHAT'S ONE MORE LANGUAGE?

Jeni Li Shoecraft has always enjoyed learning new languages. She studied Latin, German, French, and Spanish in high school and college, and she is currently learning Japanese. All this prepared her to think and communicate in new ways. When it came time to study computer programming languages, Shoecraft was ready and willing to add some new ones to her résumé.

FINDING A FUTURE

Along with discovering a natural affinity for languages there, high school was the place where Shoecraft fell in love with computers. This discovery actually came in a roundabout way. She'd taken a computer typing class, liked the teacher, and really liked one of the boys in the class. Given the option to take a computer programming class the next semester, she took it. By the end of the semester the boy was history, but computers were her destiny.

About that same time, Shoecraft's father decided she needed a job and hired her to do data entry in his office. It was boring work, but when Shoecraft discovered a glitch in the system, she got the chance to write—for pay for the first time—a program to fix it. Now that's initiative!

ONE MINUTE SHE WAS DANCING . . .

While in college, one of Shoecraft's favorite ways to relax after a day in class was to attend dance jams—no drinking, no smoking, just lots of great dancing. One night she met someone, and they began talking about their mutual interest in computers. He set up an interview with his boss, and the next thing Shoecraft knew, she had a job in sales and technical support for a small computer firm. The position provided just the experience she needed to augment her computer science degree and help her land a position in the computer division of Arizona State University (ASU).

ON TO BIGGER AND BETTER THINGS

The ASU job involved providing computer support for faculty and staff at the west campus as well as installing software, training, and writing documentation for computer users. It was fun and interesting work. But, since her goal at any job is to work herself out of a position, she soon found many ways to help the staff help themselves, which left more time for other fun and interesting work. In her spare time she discovered the World Wide Web and loved it. So she taught herself enough HTML to create a personal website.

THE RIGHT PLACE AT THE RIGHT TIME

Perfect timing came into play at this point. Shoecraft was hooked on the Web and getting pretty good at finding her way around the system. At the same time, her department was asked to develop an interactive project for the university's internal web, and Shoecraft's boss tapped her newfound skill for the task. The first project was a hit with the boss and with Shoecraft. On the project, she worked hard to develop a good relationship with the university web staff, which made working together a breeze when she became campus webmaster.

Being close to the university web staff also meant that Shoecraft was one of the first to know when a web position became available 35 miles closer to home at a different ASU campus. The end result of all her effort was that she worked herself right into a brand-new position as webmaster for the ASU website.

The moral of the story behind Shoecraft's interesting career progression is that you should keep learning and stay a step ahead of your current position. You just never know where this path will lead, but it tends to offer a beeline toward better opportunities.

MAKE A COMPUTER DETOUR!

Computers are entering every area of life and work. This book has given you an overview of a few ways in which compouters are being used. But there are thousands more. The following list provides some more ideas for making computers a focal point of your career. These ideas are grouped in categories to help you narrow down specific interest areas. Use them as a starting point to search out the best spot for yoru computer interests and abilities.

To make the most of this phase of your exploration, draw up a list of the ideas that you'd like to learn more about. Look them up in a career encyclopedia and get acquainted with more possibilities for your future!

When you come across a particularly intriguing occupation, use the form on page 133 to record your discoveries.

A WORLD OF COMPUTER CAREERS

HARDWARE
These professions involve working with the "guts" of the computer, developing bigger and better technology that continues to revolutionize the workplace. Innovation, computer expertise, and logical thinking are common traits of all kinds of hardware professionals.

computer chip designer
computer chip manufacturing
  technician
computer designer

computer development engineer
electrical engineer
manufacturing engineer
semiconductor engineer

SOFTWARE
Software professionals do the thinking behind everything a computer does, from very simple commands to extremely complicated computerized tasks. Creativity, the ability to break complex tasks into minute steps, and effective communication skills are important assets for most types of software professionals.

CD-ROM producer
computer game animator
computer game programmer
database designer
entertainment software writer
freelance computer programmer
graphical user interface designer

quality assurance manager
software engineer
software integration engineer
software project manager
software tester
software tools developer
virtual reality developer

SERVICES FOR COMPUTER USERS
Computer service occupations tend to blend equal parts of computer expertise and communication skills. In various ways, they help users maximize the potential of their computer systems.

computer consultant
computer science teacher
computer service bureau
  manager

cyberlibrarian
data retrieval specialist
freelance technical writer

INFORMATION SYSTEMS MANAGEMENT

Working with lots of information and lots of computer power summarizes what's involved in information systems management. These professionals must have exceptional computer skills as well as the ability to manage other people, information, and technology.

database administrator
manager of information
  systems (MIS)

network manager
systems administrator
systems integrator

NETWORK AND ON-LINE SERVICES

The opportunities in this arena continue to grow. The more uses people find for the Internet, the more work there will be to keep things running smoothly.

Internet access provider
Internet promotions consultant
Internet service provider
  systems administrator
Internet storefront operator

intranet specialist
local area network (LAN)
  specialist
systems operator (SYSOP)
web server administrator

SALES AND INFORMATION SERVICES

These options provide some ways to blend an interest in computers with other types of talent. Whether it's a gift for gab or a way with the written word, there's a way to put it to work here.

computer book author
computer book editor
computer consultant recruiter
computer industry reporter
computer magazine writer

computer sales representative
computer store owner
public relations manager
software industry analyst
trade show promoter

COMPUTER-RELYING JOBS—
SPECIALIZED AND NONSPECIALIZED

The possibilities here are endless. Virtually any type of business or industry has been touched in one way or another by computers. See how many other ideas you can add to this list.

aircraft designer
artist
automobile designer
cable network digital system
    analyst
CAD (computer-aided design)
    illustrator
CAD manager
CAM (computer-aided
    manufacture) engineer
cartoonist
computer animator
computer musician
consumer product research
data entry clerk

desktop publisher
electronic publisher
graphic designer
MIDI (musical instrument
    digital interface) engineer
newsletter publisher
printing typesetter
receptionist
reservations clerk
secretary
virtual reality entertainment
    center operator
word processor operator
zine publisher

INFORMATION
IS POWER

Mind-boggling, isn't it? There are so many great choices, so many jobs you've never heard of before. How will you ever narrow it down to the perfect spot for you?

First, pinpoint the ideas that sound the most interesting to you. Then, find out all you can about them. As you may have noticed, a similar pattern of information was used for each of the career entries featured in this book. Each entry included

- 🔆 a general description or definition of the career
- 🔆 some hands-on projects that give readers a chance to actually experience a job
- 🔆 a list of organizations to contact for more information
- 🔆 an interview with a professional

You can use information like this to help you determine the best career path to pursue. Since there isn't room in one book to profile all these computer career choices, here's your chance to do it yourself. Conduct a full investigation into a computer career that interests you.

Please Note: If this book does not belong to you use a separate sheet of paper to record your responses to the following questions.

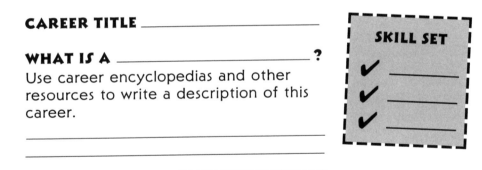

CAREER TITLE _____

WHAT IS A _____ **?**
Use career encyclopedias and other resources to write a description of this career.

_____
_____
_____

SKILL SET
✔ _____
✔ _____
✔ _____

TRY IT OUT
Write project ideas here. Ask your parents and your teacher to come up with a plan.

_____
_____
_____

CHECK IT OUT

List professional organizations where you can learn more about this profession.

_____
_____
_____

GET ACQUAINTED

Interview a professional in the field and summarize your findings.

_____
_____
_____

DON'T STOP NOW!

GO FOR IT!

It's been a fast-paced trip so far. Take a break, regroup, and look at all the progress you've made.

1st Stop: Self-Discovery
You discovered some personal interests and natural abilities that you can start building a career around.

2nd Stop: Exploration
You've explored an exciting array of career opportunities in computers. You're now aware that your career can involve either a specialized area with many educational requirements or that it can involve a practical application of computer science methods with a minimum of training and experience.

At this point, you've found a couple of (or few) careers that really intrigue you. Now it's time to put it all together and do all you can to make an informed, intelligent choice. It's time to move on.

3rd Stop: Experimentation

By the time you finish this section, you'll have reached one of three points in the career planning process.

1. **Green light!** You found it. No need to look any further. This is *the* career for you. (This may happen to a lucky few. Don't worry if it hasn't happened yet for you. This whole process is about exploring options, experimenting with ideas, and, eventually, making the best choice for you.)

2. **Yellow light!** Close, but not quite. You seem to be on the right path but you haven't nailed things down for sure. (This is where many people your age end up, and it's a good place to be. You've learned what it takes to really check things out. Hang in there. Your time will come.)

3. **Red light!** Whoa! No doubt about it, this career just isn't for you. (Congratulations! Aren't you glad you found out now and not after you'd spent four years in college preparing for this career? Your next stop: Make a U-turn and start this process over with another career.)

Here's a sneak peek at what you'll be doing in the next section.

☼ First, you'll pick a favorite career idea (or two or three).

☼ Second, you'll snoop around the library to find answers to the 10 things you've just got to know about your future career.

☼ Third, you'll pick up the phone and talk to someone whose career you admire to find out what it's really like.

☼ Fourth, you'll link up with a whole world of great information about your career idea on the Internet (it's easier than you think).

☼ Fifth, you'll go on the job to shadow a professional for a day.

Hang on to your hats and get ready to make tracks!

#1 NARROW DOWN YOUR CHOICES

You've been introduced to quite a few computer career ideas. You may also have some ideas of your own to add. Which ones appeal to you the most?

Write your top three choices in the spaces below. (Sorry if this is starting to sound like a broken record, but . . . if this book does not belong to you, write your responses on a separate sheet of paper.)

1. _____
2. _____
3. _____

#2 SNOOP AT THE LIBRARY

Take your list of favorite career ideas, a notebook, and a helpful adult with you to the library. When you get there, go to the reference section and ask the librarian to help you find

books about careers. Most libraries will have at least one set of career encyclopedias. Some of the larger libraries may also have career information on CD-ROM.

Gather all the information you can and use it to answer the following questions in your notebook about each of the careers on your list. Make sure to ask for help if you get stuck.

TOP 10 THINGS YOU NEED TO KNOW ABOUT YOUR CAREER

1. What kinds of skills does this job require?
2. What kind of training is required? (Compare the options for a high school degree, trade school degree, two-year degree, four-year degree, and advanced degree.)
3. What types of classes do I need to take in high school in order to be accepted into a training program?
4. What are the names of three schools or colleges where I can get the training I need?
5. Are there any apprenticeship or internship opportunities available? If so, where? If not, could I create my own opportunity? How?
6. How much money can I expect to earn as a beginner? How much with more experience?
7. What kinds of places hire people to do this kind of work?
8. What is a typical work environment like? For example, would I work in a busy office, outdoors, or in a laboratory?
9. What are some books and magazines I could read to learn more about this career? Make a list and look for them at your library.
10. Where can I write for more information? Make a list of professional associations.

#3 CHAT ON THE PHONE

Talking to a seasoned professional—someone who experiences the job day in and day out—can be a great way to get the inside story on what a career is all about. Fortunately for you, the experts in any career field can be as close as the nearest telephone.

Sure it can be a bit scary calling up an adult whom you don't know. But, two things are in your favor:

1. They can't see you. The worst thing they can do is hang up on you, so just relax and enjoy the conversation.
2. They'll probably be happy to talk to you about their job. In fact, most people will be flattered that you've called. If you happen to contact someone who seems reluctant to talk, thank them for their time and try someone else.

Here are a few pointers to help make your telephone interview a success.

- ☼ Mind your manners and speak clearly.
- ☼ Be respectful of their time and position.
- ☼ Be prepared with good questions and take notes as you talk.

One more commonsense reminder: Be careful about giving out your address and DO NOT arrange to meet anyone you don't know without your parents' supervision.

TRACKING DOWN CAREER EXPERTS

You might be wondering by now how to find someone to interview. Have no fear! It's easy, if you're persistent. All you have to do is ask. Ask the right people and you'll have a great lead in no time.

A few of the people to ask and sources to turn to are

Your parents. They may know someone (or know someone who knows someone) who has just the kind of job you're looking for.

Your friends and neighbors. You might be surprised to find out how many interesting jobs these people have when you start asking them what they (or their parents) do for a living.

Librarians. Since you've already figured out what kinds of companies employ people in your field of interest, the next step is to ask for information about local employers. Although it's a bit cumbersome to use, a big volume called *Contacts Influential* can provide this kind of information.

Professional associations. Call or write to the professional associations you discovered in Activity #1 a few pages back and ask for recommendations.

Chambers of commerce. The local chamber of commerce probably has a directory of employers, their specialties, and their phone numbers. Call the chamber, explain what you are looking for, and give the person a chance to help the future workforce.

Newspaper and magazine articles. Find an article about the subject you are interested in. Chances are pretty good that it will mention the name of at least one expert in the field. The article probably won't include the person's phone number (that would be too easy), so you'll have to look for clues. Common clues include the name of the company that the expert works for, the town that he or she lives in, and if the person is an author, the name of his or her publisher. Make a few phone calls and track the person down (if long distance calls are involved, make sure to get your parents' permission first).

INQUIRING KIDS WANT TO KNOW

Before you make the call, make a list of questions to ask. You'll cover more ground if you focus on using the five *w*'s (and the *h*) that you've probably heard about in your creative writing classes: Who? What? Where? When? How? and Why? For example,

1. Who do you work for?
2. What is a typical work day like for you?
3. Where can I get some on-the-job experience?
4. When did you become a _____?
   (profession)
5. How much can you earn in this profession? (But, remember it's not polite to ask someone how much *he* or *she* earns.)
6. Why did you choose this profession?

One last suggestion: Add a professional (and very classy) touch to the interview process by following up with a thank-you note to the person who took time out of a busy schedule to talk with you.

#4 SURF THE NET

With the Internet, the new information super-highway, charging full steam ahead, you literally have a world of information at your fingertips. The Internet has something for everyone, and it's getting easier to access all the time. An increasing number of libraries and schools are offering access to the Internet on their computers. In addition, companies such as America Online and CompuServe have made it possible for anyone with a home computer to surf the World Wide Web.

A typical career search will land everything from the latest news on developments in the field and course notes from universities to museum exhibits, interactive games, educational activities, and more. You just can't beat the timeliness or the variety of information available on the Net.

One of the easiest ways to track down this information is to use an Internet search engine, such as Yahoo! Simply type in the topic you are looking for, and in a matter of seconds, you'll have a list of options from around the world. It's fun to browse—you never know what you'll come up with.

To narrow down your search a bit, look for specific websites, forums, or chatrooms that are related to your topic in the following publications:

Hahn, Harley. *The Internet Yellow Pages.* Berkeley, Calif.: Osborne McGraw Hill, 1997.
———. *The World Wide Web Yellow Pages.* Berkeley, Calif.: Osborne McGraw Hill, 1997.

To go on-line at home you may want to compare two of the more popular on-line services: America Online and CompuServe. Please note that there is a monthly subscription fee for using these services. There can also be extra fees attached to specific forums and services, so *make sure you have your parents' OK before you sign up.* For information about America Online call 800-827-6364. For information about CompuServe call 800-848-8990. Both services frequently offer free start-up deals, so shop around.

There are also many other services, depending on where you live. Check your local phone book or ads in local computer magazines for other service options.

Before you link up, keep in mind that many of these sites are geared toward professionals who are already working in a particular field. Some of the sites can get pretty technical. Just use the experience as a chance to nose around the field, hang out with the people who are tops in the field, and think about whether or not you'd like to be involved in a profession like that.

Specific sites to look for are the following:

Professional associations. Find out about what's happening in the field, conferences, journals, and other helpful tidbits.

Schools that specialize in this area. Many include research tools, introductory courses, and all kinds of interesting information.

Government agencies. Quite a few are going high-tech with lots of helpful resources.

Websites hosted by experts in the field (this seems to be a popular hobby among many professionals). These websites are often as entertaining as they are informative.

If you're not sure where to go, just start clicking around. Sites often link to other sites. You may want to jot down notes about favorite sites. Sometimes you can even print out information that isn't copyright-protected; try the print option and see what happens.

Be prepared: Surfing the Internet can be an addicting habit! There is so much great information. It's a fun way to focus on your future.

#5 SHADOW A PROFESSIONAL

Linking up with someone who is gainfully employed in a profession that you want to explore is a great way to find out what a career is like. Following someone around while the person is at work is called "shadowing." Try it!

This process involves three steps.

1. Find someone to shadow. Some suggestions include
   - the person you interviewed (if you enjoyed talking with him or her and feel comfortable about asking the person to show you around the workplace)
   - friends and neighbors (you may even be shocked to discover that your parents have interesting jobs)
   - workers at the chamber of commerce may know of mentoring programs available in your area (it's a popular concept, so most larger areas should have something going on)
   - someone at your local School-to-Work office, the local Boy Scouts Explorer program director (this is available to girls too!), or your school guidance counselor
2. Make a date. Call and make an appointment. Find out when is the best time for arrival and departure. Make arrangements with a parent or other respected adult to go with you and get there on time.
3. Keep your ears and eyes open. This is one time when it is OK to be nosy. Ask questions. Notice everything that is happening around you. Ask your host to let you try some of the tasks he or she is doing.

The basic idea of the shadowing experience is to put yourself in the other person's shoes and see how they fit. Imagine yourself having a job like this 10 or 15 years down the road. It's a great way to find out if you are suited for a particular line of work.

BE CAREFUL OUT THERE!

Two cautions must accompany this recommendation. First, remember the stranger danger rules of your childhood. NEVER meet with anyone you don't know without your parents' permission and ALWAYS meet in a supervised situation—at the office or with your parents.

Second, be careful not to overdo it. These people are busy earning a living, so respect their time by limiting your contact and coming prepared with valid questions and background information.

PLAN B

If shadowing opportunities are limited where you live, try one of these approaches for learning the ropes from a professional.

Pen pals. Find a mentor who is willing to share information, send interesting materials, or answer specific questions that come up during your search.

Cyber pals. Go on-line in a forum or chatroom related to your profession. You'll be able to chat with professionals from all over the world.

If you want to get some more on-the-job experience, try one of these approaches.

Volunteer to do the dirty work. Volunteer to work for someone who has a job that interests you for a specified period of time. Do anything—filing, errands, emptying trash cans—that puts you in contact with professionals. Notice every tiny detail about the profession. Listen to the lingo they use in the profession. Watch how they perform their jobs on a day-to-day basis.

Be an apprentice. This centuries-old job training method is making a comeback. Find out if you can set up an official on-the-job training program to gain valuable experience. Ask professional associations about apprenticeship opportunities. Once again, a School-to-Work program can be a great asset. In many areas, they've established some very interesting career training opportunities.

Hire yourself for the job. Maybe you are simply too young to do much in the way of on-the-job training right now. That's OK. Start learning all you can now and you'll be ready to really wow them when the time is right. Make sure you do all the Try It Out activities included for the career(s) you are most interested in. Use those activities as a starting point for creating other projects that will give you a feel for what the job is like.

WHAT'S NEXT?

Have you carefully worked your way through all of the suggested activities? You haven't tried to sneak past anything, have you? This isn't a place for shortcuts. If you've done the activities, you're ready to decide where you stand with each career idea. So what is it? Green light? See page 150. Yellow light? See page 149. Red light? See page 148. Find the spot that best describes your response to what you've discovered about this career idea and plan your next move.

RED LIGHT

So you've decided this career is definitely not for you—hang in there! The process of elimination is an important one. You've learned some valuable career planning skills; use them to explore other ideas. In the meantime, use the following road map to chart a plan to get beyond this "spinning your wheels" point in the process.

Take a variety of classes at school to expose yourself to new ideas and expand the options. Make a list of courses you want to try.

🔅 _____
🔅 _____
🔅 _____
🔅 _____

Get involved in clubs and other after-school activities (like 4-H or Boy Scout Explorers) to further develop your interests. Write down some that interest you.

🔅 _____
🔅 _____
🔅 _____
🔅 _____

Read all you can find about interesting people and their work. Make a list of people you'd like to learn more about.

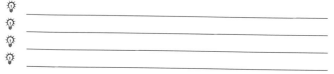

🔅 _____
🔅 _____
🔅 _____
🔅 _____

Keep at it. Time is on your side. Finding the perfect work for you is worth a little effort. Once you've crossed this hurdle, move on to the next pages and continue mapping out a great future.

YELLOW LIGHT

Proceed with caution. While the idea continues to intrigue you, you may wonder if it's the best choice for you. Your concerns are legitimate (listen to that nagging little voice inside!).

Maybe it's the training requirements that intimidate you. Maybe you have concerns about finding a good job once you complete the training. Maybe you wonder if you have what it takes to do the job.

At this point, it's good to remember that there is often more than one way to get somewhere. Check out all the choices and choose the route that's best for you. Use the following road map to move on down the road in your career planning adventure.

Make two lists. On the first, list the things you like most about the career you are currently investigating. On the second, list the things that are most important to you in a future career. Look for similarities on both lists and focus on careers that emphasize these similar key points.

Current Career	Future Career
☼ _____	☼ _____
☼ _____	☼ _____

What are some career ideas that are similar to the one you have in mind? Find out all you can about them. Go back through the exploration process explained on pages 137 to 146 and repeat some of the exercises that were most valuable.

☼ _____
☼ _____
☼ _____
☼ _____

Visit your school counselor and ask him or her which career assessment tools are available through your school. Use these to find out more about your strengths and interests. List the date, time, and place for any assessment tests you plan to take.

- _____
- _____
- _____
- _____

What other adults do you know and respect to whom you can talk about your future? They may have ideas that you've never thought of.

- _____
- _____
- _____
- _____

What kinds of part-time jobs, volunteer work, or after-school experiences can you look into that will give you a chance to build your skills and test your abilities? Think about how you can tap into these opportunities.

- _____
- _____
- _____
- _____

GREEN LIGHT

Yahoo! You are totally turned on to this career idea and ready to do whatever it takes to make it your life's work. Go for it!

Find out what kinds of classes you need to take now to prepare for this career. List them here.

- _____
- _____
- _____
- _____

What are some on-the-job training possibilities for you to pursue? List the company name, a person to contact, and the phone number.

- ☼ _____
- ☼ _____
- ☼ _____
- ☼ _____

Find out if there are any internship or apprenticeship opportunities available in this career field. List contacts and phone numbers.

- ☼ _____
- ☼ _____
- ☼ _____
- ☼ _____

What kind of education will you need after you graduate from high school? Describe the options.

- ☼ _____
- ☼ _____
- ☼ _____
- ☼ _____

No matter what the educational requirements are, the better your grades are during junior and senior high school, the better your chances for the future.

Take a minute to think about some areas that need improvement in your schoolwork. Write your goals for giving it all you've got here.

- ☼ _____
- ☼ _____
- ☼ _____
- ☼ _____

Where can you get the training you'll need? Make a list of colleges, technical schools, or vocational programs. Include addresses so that you can write to request a catalog.

- 💡 _____
- 💡 _____
- 💡 _____
- 💡 _____

HOORAY! YOU DID IT!

This has been quite a trip. If someone tries to tell you that this process is easy, don't believe it. Figuring out what you want to do with the rest of your life is heavy stuff, and it should be. If you don't put some thought (and some sweat and hard work) into the process, you'll get stuck with whatever comes your way. Make sure you make the most of your potential.

You may not have things planned to a T. Actually, it's probably better if you don't. You'll change some of your ideas as you grow and experience new things. And, you may find an interesting detour or two along the way. That's OK.

The most important thing about beginning this process now is that you've started to dream. You've discovered that you have some unique talents and abilities to share. You've become aware of some of the ways you can use them to make a living—and, perhaps, make a difference in the world.

Whatever you do, don't lose sight of the hopes and dreams you've discovered. You've got your entire future ahead of you. Use it wisely.

SOME FUTURE DESTINATIONS

Wow! You've really made tracks during this whole process. Now that you've gotten this far, you'll want to keep moving forward to a great future. This section will point you toward some useful resources to help you make a conscientious career choice (that's just the opposite of falling into any old job on a fluke).

IT'S NOT JUST FOR NERDS

The school counselor's office is not just a place where teachers send troublemakers. One of its main purposes is to help students like you make the most of your educational opportunities. Most schools will have a number of useful resources, including career assessment tools (ask about the Self-Directed Search Career Explorer or the COPS Interest

Inventory—these are especially useful assessments for people your age). There may also be a stash of books, videos, and other helpful materials.

Make sure no one's looking and sneak into your school counseling office to get some expert advice!

AWESOME INTERNET CAREER RESOURCES

Your parents will be green with envy when they see all the career planning resources you have at your fingertips. Get ready to hear them whine, "But they didn't have all this stuff when I was a kid." Make the most of these cyberspace opportunities.

- ☆ The Career Center for Teens (a site sponsored by Public Television Outreach) includes activities and information on 21st-century career opportunities. Find it at http://www.pbs.org/jobs/teenindex.html.
- ☆ Future Scan includes in-depth profiles on a wide variety of career choices and expert advice from their "Guidance Gurus." Check it out at http://www.future-scan.com.
- ☆ Just for fun visit the Jam!z Knowzone Careers page and chat with other kids about your career dreams. You'll find them by going to http://www.jamz.com and clicking on the KnowZone icon. (Note: This site is monitored!)
- ☆ JobSmart's Career Guides is another site to explore specific career choices. Look for it at http://www.jobsmart.org/tools/career/spec-car.htm.

IT'S NOT JUST FOR BOYS

Boys and girls alike are encouraged to contact their local version of the Boy Scouts Explorer program. It offers exciting on-the-job training experiences in a variety of professional fields. Look in the white pages of your community phone book for the local Boy Scouts of America program.

MORE CAREER BOOKS ESPECIALLY FOR COMPUTER WHIZZES

Anything having to do with computers promises plenty of opportunity well into the next century. The following books provide more information about computer-related career options.

Bone, Jan. *Opportunities in Computer-Aided Design and Computer Aided Manufacturing.* Lincolnwood, Ill. VGM Career Horizons, 1993.

Burns, Julie Kling. *Opportunities in Computer Systems Careers.* Lincolnwood, Ill.: VGM Career Horizons, 1996.

Eberts, Marjorie, and Margaret Gisler. *Careers for Computer Buffs and Other Technological Types.* Lincolnwood, Ill.: VGM Career Horizons, 1996.

Edwards, Paul, and Sarah Edwards. *Making Money with Your Computer at Home.* New York: Putnam, 1993.

Goldstein, Harold, and Bryna S. Fraser. *Getting a Job in the Computer Age.* Princeton, N.J.: Peterson's Guides, Inc., 1986.

Hawkins, Lori, and Betsy Dowling. *100 Jobs in Technology.* New York: Macmillan, 1996.

Kanter, Elliott S. *Opportunities in Computer Maintenance Careers.* Lincolnwood, Ill.: VGM Career Horizons, 1995.

Kling, Julie L. *Opportunities in Computer Science Careers.* Lincolnwood, Ill.: NTC Publishing Group, 1991.

Krause, David. *Get the Best Jobs in DP: The Computer Professional's Technical Interview Guide.* Edmonds, Wash.: Mind Management, 1989.

Morgan, Bradley J., and Joseph M. Palmisano. *Computer and Software Design Career Directory.* Detroit: Gale Research, Inc., 1993.

Peterson's Job Opportunities for Engineering, Science and Computer Graduates. Princeton, N.J.: Peterson's Guides, 1993.

Ruhl, Janet Lehrman. *The Programmer's Survival Guide: Career Strategies for Computer Professionals.* Old Tappan, N.J.: Prentice Hall, 1988.

Spencer, Jean W. *Exploring Careers as a Computer Technician.* New York: Rosen Publishing Group, 1989.

William, Linda. *Careers Without College: Computers.* Princeton, N.J.: Peterson's Guides, 1992.

HEAVY-DUTY RESOURCES

Career encyclopedias provide general information about a lot of professions and can be a great place to start a career search. Those listed here are easy to use and provide useful information about nearly a zillion different jobs. Look for them in the reference section of your local library.

Cosgrove, Holli, ed. *Career Discovery Encyclopedia: 1997 Edition*. Chicago: J. G. Ferguson Publishing Company, 1997.

Encyclopedia of Career Choices for the 1990's. New York: Perigee Books/Putnam Publishing Group, 1992.

Maze, Marilyn, Donald Mayall, and J. Michael Farr. *The Enhanced Guide for Occupational Exploration: Descriptions for the 2,500 Most Important Jobs*. Indianapolis: JIST, 1995.

VGM's Careers Encyclopedia. Lincolnwood, Ill.: VGM Career Books, 1997.

FINDING PLACES TO WORK

Use resources like these to find leads on local businesses, mentors, job shadowing opportunities, and internships. Later, use these same resources to find a great job!

Job Bank Guide to Computer Companies. Holbrook, Mass.: Adams Media Group, 1997.

Job Opportunities in Engineering and Technology, 1997. Princeton, N.J.: Peterson's Guides, Inc., 1997.

Lanthrop, Richard. *Who's Hiring Who?* Berkeley, Calif.: Ten Speed Press, 1989.

LeCompte, Michelle. *Job Hunter's Sourcebook: Where to Find Employment Leads and Other Job Search Resources*. Detroit: Gale Research Inc., 1996.

FINDING PLACES TO PRACTICE JOB SKILLS

An apprenticeship is an official opportunity to learn a specific profession by working side by side with a skilled professional. As a training method, it's as old as the hills, and it's making a comeback in a big way because people are realizing that doing a job is simply the best way to learn a job.

An internship is an official opportunity to gain work experience (paid or unpaid) in an industry of interest. Interns are more likely to be given entry-level tasks but often have the chance to rub elbows with people in key positions within a company. In comparison to an apprenticeship, which offers very detailed training for a specific job, an internship offers a broader look at a particular kind of work environment.

Both are great ways to learn the ropes and stay one step ahead of the competition. Consider it dress rehearsal for the real thing!

Cantrell, Will. *International Internships and Volunteer Programs.* Oakton, Va.: World Wise Books, 1992.

Guide to Apprenticeship Programs for Non-College Bound Youth. New York: Rosen, 1996.

Hepburn, Diane, ed. *Internships 1997.* Princeton, N.J.: Peterson's, 1997.

Summerfield, Carol J., and Holli Cosgrove. *Ferguson's Guide to Apprenticeship Programs: Traditional and Nontraditional.* Chicago: Ferguson's, 1994.

NO-COLLEGE OCCUPATIONS

Some of you will be relieved to learn that a college degree is not the only route to a satisfying, well-paying career. Whew! If you'd rather skip some of the schooling and get down to work, here are some books you need to consult.

Abrams, Kathleen. S. *Guide to Careers Without College.* Danbury, Conn.: Franklin Watts, 1995.

Corwen Leonard. *College Not Required!: 100 Great Careers That Don't Require a College Degree.* New York: Macmillan, 1995.

Farr, J. Michael. *America's Top Jobs for People Without College Degrees.* Indianapolis: JIST, 1997.

Jakubiak, J. *Specialty Occupational Outlook: Trade and Technical.* Detroit: Gale Research Inc., 1996.

Unger, Harlow G. *But What If I Don't Want to Go to College?: A Guide to Successful Careers through Alternative Education.* Rev. ed. New York: Facts On File, 1998.

Williams, Linda. *Careers Without College: Computers.* Princeton, N.J.: Peterson's Guides, Inc., 1997.

INDEX

Page numbers in **boldface** indicate main articles. Page numbers in *italics* indicate photographs.